Published by EVB Press www.evbpress.com United Kingdom

Copyright 2016 EVB Press except where individual authors are listed. Copyright remains with individual authors whose name appears at the heading of the section. Written permission must be given before reproducing any part of this book in whole or in part, except that which is legally permitted under UK Copyright law.

All Rights Reserved

Manufactured in the United Kingdom

For permission to reproduce any material in this book contact EVB Press at

www.evbpress.com

ISBN: 978-1-910748-09-1
(paperback)

ISBN: 978-1-910748-10-7
(Kindle)

Acknowledgements

A Room of Our Own: A Feminist/ Womanist Network is a women-only platform created to share women's fiction, poetry, art, essays, rants and musings. It was created both to combat cultural femicide – the term coined by feminist writer Bidisha to define the erasure of women from politics, art, and culture – and celebrate women's creativity in a space without men.

Women-only spaces are a fundamental part of the feminist movement and represent women's right to self-determination and liberation. As Andrea Dworkin wrote in her seminal text Intercourse :

"Men often react to women's words – speaking and writing – as if they were acts of violence; sometimes men react to women's words with violence. So we lower our voices. Women whisper. Women apologize. Women shut up. Women trivialize what we know. Women shrink. Women pull back. Most women have experienced enough dominance from men – control, violence, insult, contempt – that no threat seems empty."

I have been online for nearly 20 years and the abuse of women online has become worse. The misogynistic attacks on feminists like Zoë Quinn, Anita Sarkeesian, Feminista Jones – and every single other feminist who dares to speak publicly about male violence, street harassment and video games – are targeted to silence women. Twitter, Facebook and other social media platforms have done very little to deal with abusive behaviour, prioritising profits over the safety of their users.

In many ways, Dworkin's words are an understatement of what occurs online. Men's reactions to women's words have become more violent, more hateful, in many ways, more socially acceptable. Women can't hear one another when we're forced to plough through thousands of threats of rape, torture and death in online spaces. We lock our Twitter accounts, censor ourselves and hope we don't become the next target. We don't need a threat to be directed at us personally for it to act as a silencing tactic.

This is the reality in which A Room of Our Own was born. I wanted to create a space for feminists by feminists – a safe space where women can share their thoughts, their writing, their art and their lives without abusive comments and without men dictating the terms of the discussion. The need for this space is seen daily in the number of abusive comments I delete from men and the number I have to block on Twitter. More importantly, the women involved have spoken about how significant the space is to them – that an online space where men's entitlement to women's time is simply not accepted makes a difference. A space which prioritises women's voices over men's, that refuses to allow men to dictate the terms of the conversation and that gives a platform for all feminists to speak is essential to the health and breadth of the feminist movement.

It doesn't matter what you blog about – hockey, parenting, donuts or feminist theory – as long as you are a feminist or womanist, you are welcome here. We expect that members will have fundamentally different definitions of feminism and womanism. We believe these differences are worth exploring, debating and celebrating.

A Room of Our Own is open to all feminists and womanists because our voices matter; because we have value and because we will change the world.

This project would not exist without the support and encouragement of Cath Andrews, Alison Boydell, Cath Elliot, Karen Ingala Smith, Jo Costello, Cath Costello, Barbara Hughes, Portia Smart, Cat Eleven, Ericka Garrett, Lorrie Hartshorn, Liz Kelly, Lynn Schreiber, Millie Slavidou, Katharine Edgar, and Lucy Allen.

A huge thank you to all the women who donated their writing to make this anthology possible: Susan Dunsford, Lucy Middlemass, Lorrie Hartshorn, Estella Muzito, Egoyibo Okoro, Laura Rimmer, Poppy O'Neill, Ericka Garrett, Cath Bore, Claire Heuchan, Priscilla Lugo, Durre Mughal, Sunayna Pal, Christina Paschyn, Effie Samara, and Millie Slavidou. And a second thank you to Lucy Middlemass for donating her time to edit this anthology.

Contents

Room For Our Dangerous Ideas   6

Hair by Poppy O'Neill   7

Used Goods by Durre Mughal   11

Celeste by Lucy Middlemass   13

Practicing Self-Love by Priscilla Lugo   45

Room For Our Courage   47

Prologue/Epilogue by Lorrie Hartshorn   48

Your Silence Will Not Protect You: Racism in the Feminist Movement by Claire Heuchan   49

An Indian woman by Sunayna Pal   54

The Outsider Within: Racism in the Feminist Movement by Claire Heuchan   56

Abortion by Erika Garrett   61

Room For Our Anger   62

Cyborg by Susan Dunsford   63

You women! You're such bitches by Cath Bore   65

The Colour of Justice by Estella Muzito   67

Room For Ourselves   72

Sister, mother by Lorrie Hartshorn   73

Because Ogwugwu Said So by Egoyibo Okoro   75

Giving birth in a dictatorship by Erika Garrett   80

Feminist Mothering with Fibromyalgia by Louise Pennington   83

Room For Our Escape   86

Hollywood's Woman Problem in Action Films by Christina Paschyn   88

Room For Our Future   97

What's in a Word? by Millie Slavidou   98

Mother's Lament by Susan Dunford   101

An Open Letter to Our Immigrant Parents by Priscilla Lugo   103

Being Chicana in College by Priscilla Lugo   105

Love Sick by Erika Garrett   107

Room For Our Knowledge 109

I am not your Mami by Priscilla Lugo 110

Understanding Feminist Standpoints: Situated Knowledges of Gender, Race, and Class Inequality by Egoyibo Okoro 113

Hysteria in Performance: The subversive potential of performative malady by Effie Samara 118

My Mother Said by Durre Mughal 128

Room For Our Dangerous Ideas

Hair by Poppy O'Neill

Before she could dismiss it as coincidence, Anna had started a new collection. She kept finding hair in her front garden. Not just a fine, static coating of cat hair, or a greasy pinch of pubes but tails, wigs, braids knotted with grosgrain ribbon.

She snatched up a tangled blonde beehive from the step and kicked the door closed behind her, mottled glass rattling in the old wooden frame. If Anna had been predisposed to a more popular hobby—crochet, genealogy, five-a-side football—then she might not have collected the little omens. She might have marched them to the wheelie bin in a pair of rusty tongs, or left a passive-aggressive note in a polythene folder tied to the gate.

But Anna was not that sort of person. Anna was ready and willing to receive each and every sign the universe sent her way. She looked for guidance in every coincidence, every animal she met. If she'd had human friends they might have anchored her in reality, but she managed to excuse herself from all but the most essential human contact.

She would flick through discarded newspapers—almost all of the coins in her purse were too soaked in significance to spend at the newsagent's—carefully carving out her horoscope (Virgo) with a pocket knife, and noting down auspicious dates on her kitchen calendar. She never walked under ladders, always picked up pennies and made sure the handles of her mugs were all facing east when she went to bed.

The tail had been first. Not a bloody, severed tail (although, of course, once it had been) but a gleaming sliver of mink, rendered into a fine decorative object by an Italian furrier. Anna had picked it up in wonder, raking her fingers through the thick, glossy fur.

She found it on the gate post, hanging from a brass ring sewn into the tailhead. Her cat, Stray, was weaving his tortoiseshell body in and out of her legs, pressing his warm, vibrating head into Anna's calves.

"What shall we do with this?" Anna said aloud, looking to the heavens for advice. "Best take it inside, rain's on the way."

The tail's touch was addictive: cool, almost liquid in its slippery smoothness. In the living room, Anna kept a large set of printer's drawers. Twelve narrow compartments with brass knobs, each opening to reveal a complicated grid of wooden rectangles, labelled to demark their contents.

Horoscopes: Successful

Found Pennies: sterling

Found Pennies: other

Poss. Doppelgangers

And so on and so forth. She pulled her label maker from the compartment marked Label Maker and punched in *Tails*, sliding the sticker onto an empty corner of the drawer with her thumbs.

Over the following weeks Anna grew used to being greeted each morning by a hairy gift from above. Sipping her coffee, she would peer out of her front window, parting the net curtains just enough to spot a fur coat or lustrous toupee blown in, she fancied, by Athena on the northwest wind. The radiators creaked under dew-damp sheepskin and soggy fur mittens. Her collection spread to fill half of her wardrobe and two of the drawers entirely, prompting a re-location of all holed stones, strangers' shopping lists and orphaned earrings, amongst others.

On the first day of winter, Anna opened the door to the postman.

"Something to sign for," he said. Anna signed the slip of card, looking past him for a piece of fine down or a glossy pelt for her collection. She eyed his moustache. "Thanks."

Anna turned back into the house, disappointed. She tugged open the envelope with her thumb. Chewing on a fingernail, she read the letter.

Housing Act 1988, section 21 (4)

NOTICE REQUIRING POSSESSION

She put down her coffee, letting it go cold on the mantelpiece while she looked out of the window. Anna had lived in the house for three years. She'd gone to work, come home, paid her rent, mown the lawn. She'd fed the cat, read her horoscope, organised her clippings and omens. She'd stayed up late, slept alone, slept in the same position every night. She'd sat inside during thunderstorms, planted a rosebush, watched foxes slink in and out of the woods at the end of the garden. It was the first house she had lived in by herself. She had sent down roots into its foundations, known its alcoves and cracks, creaky floorboards and loose connections.

As the three years had ticked by, Anna had become alarmed at the ease with which she was functioning in the world. Neighbours nodded at her and commented on the weather. She kept her job. Her bank account was in the black. In order to maintain this precarious normality, Anna had endeavoured to remain as she was, exactly. So if once a horoscope had led her to a piece of good luck, all horoscopes must be treasured. If the universe wanted her to get out of her bed on the left every morning, then she must do it. If someone was leaving hair in the garden, she must accept it, and decipher the message she was being sent.

Stray prowled in, stretched out gratuitously on the sofa and fell asleep. Anna knew what she had to do.

From skips and garage sales, junk shops and scrap yards, she collected wicker furniture, fencing panels, tarpaulin and fibreglass. In the woods outside her back gate, she crept after sunset to gather strong, flexible branches and scout for a perfect location.

Did Anna's neighbours suspect her? She had never given them any cause to think her strange, in her neat patterned blouses and sensible flats, she was the picture of respectable domesticity, a model tenant in a street of owner-occupiers. They would have been shocked indeed to see her, fingernails dirty, sweating as she sawed and wove, stitched and stuffed, heaving great wheelbarrow-fulls of materials from her house to the woods.

When the day of eviction arrived, Anna's landlord found the house spotless. The walls re-painted, the light bulbs changed, the curtains laundered.

Deep in the woods, Stray needled Anna's chest. She held his slim, bony body close as she walked through the trees, cracking branches under her feet as she went. Finally they came to a structure hanging a few feet off the ground from the branch of an oak. It was ovoid in shape, and sealed between its wood and twine panels with moss.

"Here we are, this is ours." Anna unzipped a fur coat she had adapted to make a front door. Stray flexed, unsure. Inside, it was roughly the size of a box bedroom, and lit from above by a lantern. Every inch was covered with hair and fur. Braided, stitched and knotted together to make a seamless, shining tapestry. Anna lay down along the curve of the wall, inhaling the heavy musk of the furs, species rubbing against species, sending up plumes of skin particles and DNA into the air. Her bones ached from the work of the past weeks. She lifted her newly muscular arm to welcome Stray in. But the cat stayed at the doorway, twitching the end of his tail from left to right.

Used Goods by Durre Mughal

You ready your body for him, using

a microscopic eye. Turning over

every pore for dust. Like a book or a dress

left behind in the attic. You're checking

whether the quality is any good.

Whether it is valuable enough

for sale at a car boot or eBay. You hope

that the next owner will need it more

than the last. You hope that this is exactly

what they had been searching for. You adorn it

with decorations, polish up the rusted paint.

Run a razor over and smooth out

the spikes. Try to make it more appealing

More desirable, but you can't cover up

the bile that floats up and out from the inside

every time you open your mouth. You wanted

to bandage up the pain when pain is shrapnel

caught in your blood that you need to draw out

before it damages your other, still functioning

organs. When pain is something you can't heal

Used Goods

with more of the same hands that turn cold,

turn hard, turn brittle. Don't you know that

what you need is in your own hands?

Celeste by Lucy Middlemass

One

I met Celeste in Dermatology. It was an unpromising start. The bus had been hot and airless, and everything about the day had made me miserable. I'd covered my arms but nothing could be done about my face. The letter said no make-up. People don't stare, if you're wondering. They look away. I left my seat too early and pressed the bell too early.

I was early. A group of porters smoked in the car park and watched my approach. Their shirts were undone to their stomachs, darkness drenched their armpits. I kept my sleeves over my hands, my shoulders up, my eyes elsewhere.

Inside the hospital, it was cooler the further I climbed from reality. A windowless world held together by a café, toilets and a cash point. I could survive its corridors and waiting rooms for days, I supposed.

I settled myself opposite a woman with the same condition as me, but I wasn't in the mood for *it could be worse*. I'd already walked past the sign for dialysis, used the ladies' toilets outside oncology. I knew how much worse it could be. Surely in sympathy, she looked at the clock behind the receptionist's window, at her phone, the wall.

I did the same. A notice reminded patients not to abuse or assault hospital staff. Security would be alerted immediately. I wondered what incident might have prompted its display, but not for long. It wasn't an engrossing read.

There were no magazines although the low table suggested that had not always been the case. Was the change for hygiene? All those skin conditions flaking and weeping, fluids transferring sure as fingerprints onto the glossy pages. It didn't bear thinking about. I'd brought my own, so I took it out of my bag, convincing myself it was easier if it lay open on my lap. Nothing to do with hiding the cover.

Another woman came in, about to change my life.

"Celeste Norris," she told the receptionist through the glass screen. She was much older than me, I could tell without looking. Abrupt. Experienced. Everything I wasn't.

I glanced up. She carried a huge bag as if the day might hold almost anything for her. Her hair bushed out like a horse's tail. She didn't do much with it, perhaps brushed it too hard with her elbow sticking out each morning. I looked away as she sat three seats from me. She blew out a loud, relieved breath as she did. Her bag took up the space between us.

The clock ticked towards my appointment time. I tried to find myself in articles I'd already read, considered a haircut that wouldn't suit me. I couldn't ignore the woman in the corner of my eye. Past her huge bag, her wide fingers flexed on her knee.

Five minutes to go, I felt her shift towards me. Her body was big enough to fill the gap. She leant too far and had to prop herself on the bag for balance. A stab of anxiety. I was too young and alone for conversation. And in a place like that. I'd only prepared myself for the doctor.

I looked at her the moment before she spoke. She was wearing a brown fleece despite the weather, and she'd probably forgotten about the charity badge pinned to the collar. She was outdoorsy, ruddy, a dog-walker no doubt. She collected things on those walks she no doubt took. A stick to beat back nettles, a pretty coloured leaf. She wore wellies in the rain, flat sandals for weekends by the sea. She didn't wear make-up even when it was allowed.

"You're all queer these days," she observed, loudly, her face upturned. The woman opposite stared right at us, lips apart. I didn't know what to do with my mouth. "Genderqueer, intersectionalist, questioning, asexual bi-trans-poly-I-don't-know-what."

"I'm sorry?" I said, not sure my politeness and the shake in my voice were walls she'd notice.

She nodded at my magazine. Her hair was greying, even then. "We were plain lesbians in my day. Dykes."

Behind the glass, the receptionist's hand hovered above the telephone, her neck outstretched and her bottom off the chair.

Would security be alerted? Which number to dial for this?

"What?" I said.

The woman rolled herself upright. "As long as you think you chose it, anything goes. There's nothing you don't support, I bet. Gender this. Sex-positive that. What I wouldn't give to go back in time."

She'd made conversation to criticise my likely politics? Despite the colour that must've rushed to my cheeks, I wasn't having it. I'd read enough by then, I could talk to a woman like that. Only the night before I'd been celebrating the end of my finals in our noisy student house. I was prepared.

"Some things are better," I said, forgetting to keep my voice down, feeling young and hot-handed. The receptionist relaxed cautiously, her hand out of sight. "We can get married now."

"My dear," the woman said, and I realised the trap I'd walked myself into, "we've only just met."

Two

My mug is cold against my hand on the window sill. I stand on tiptoes like a child, leaning to look down the street. Celeste took some persuading and now they're late. I don't know what Rowena drives but it's silent and still out there. Dark for an hour already and too overcast for stars.

It reeks of onion and garlic up here although Celeste told me to shut the kitchen door. We ate in a hurry and the dishwasher will have finished its cycle. I'd go down to empty it, but that's an end-of-the-day task and I'd be sending the wrong message.

They're so late it would've been nice if Rowena had texted, but maybe she and Ben were too busy trying to get past themselves to reach the door. She'd seemed surprised to hear from me when I contacted her online. Embarrassed, maybe, that it's been so long. A man with a dog crosses the road. It's only Alan from next door, I can tell by his shoulders and the dog's fast steps.

They'll say it was the rush hour although surely that's long over. If they took the ring road it couldn't take more than twenty minutes. Perhaps they are packing; I should have more patience. They're moving in the morning. Coming to us must have been somewhere at the bottom of their list, and if Rowena is the way I remember her, there will be a list.

A car turns the corner, its headlights rise and dip over the speedbumps. Alan complains about those bumps every time I speak to him, and he's stopped now to watch the car as if they'll feel his disapproval. It's hardly Rowena and Ben's fault, is it? It's definitely them; the car has slowed to look for house numbers.

The doorbell rings when I'm halfway down the stairs. They're in a hurry, there's more packing to be done when they get home. I jump the last two steps, my hand on the bannister. Celeste won't answer the door. She'll be where I left her, in front of the fire with a book.

"They're here," she calls when she hears me turn the latch.

I say, "I'm on it," and hope I don't sound excited but it's been so long since we've had guests like these.

Celeste

They're upon me the moment the door is open; a shot of cold air, my cheek against Rowena's scarf and her arms around me. The tang of aftershave at the back of my throat, Ben's voice saying, "I'll put these here," and a rigid box hitting my leg. With the door open our house is the only bright, warm space on the street and I realise that if I don't close it soon, every precious thing we have might just spill out.

There's a bunch of flowers in my hands with a card taped to the cellophane and a weighty gift bag it'd be impossible to mistake. My thanks are lost in Rowena telling me we live on a lovely street and that she can't wait to meet Celeste.

"You haven't changed a bit, Emma," she adds. It occurs to me it'd be funny to tell her she's wrong.

I stand back to let them in properly and somehow they and their possessions push me to the living room. Ben puts down two unwieldy carry cases that take up most of the floor.

"This is Celeste," I announce, hoping they respond to the awe in my tone. Celeste is sitting up straight by the fire. One side of her face is flushed and I can guess how they might see her. She's pale and she's pulled her blanket up. I had the front door open far too long.

"Hello," she says, friendly enough. She's doing this for me, she said she would.

"Sorry we're so late," Rowena says, taking Celeste's hand in both of hers. "It's lovely to meet you."

"You were hard to find," Ben adds. There's accusation in his voice I know Celeste won't have missed. He excuses himself, patting his coat pockets, and goes back out to the car leaving all the doors open.

Rowena tells Celeste we have a beautiful room. "It's so nice to see an open fire. It's freezing out there." She rubs her hands together and holds her palms out towards the hearth.

"It's November," Celeste says.

"Right." She frowns slightly, hiding it with her head down, then looks at me. "Lovely candles too. Such a nice touch."

"How were they in the car?" I ask, bending. Two sets of green eyes flash in the carry cases. I'd quite liked the look of them from the photos Rowena posted on Facebook. They look like witches' cats.

"Well," Rowena starts.

"Fine. They weren't bothered," Ben answers, coming back in with his trainers still on. He's got his arms full of two enormous sacks of dry food which make Celeste pull a face. I decide not to notice. He lets two plastic trays slip out of his grip and I don't blame Celeste for the look she gives those. It's not as if she'll be emptying them, though, is it?

I go to shut the front door. That's fair enough, he had so much to carry. I can hear Rowena complimenting the pictures and our overflowing bookshelves. The candles are a nice touch, she says again. It's very homely. Celeste doesn't point out the books are mostly hers, or that she wrote two of them.

There's no space for me when I come back. Rowena has taken the nearest chair and Ben is taking off his coat, arms everywhere. He hasn't changed much either, there's the hollow in his chin I noticed when he spoke to me during Freshers' Week. He has bulked up since then. He's been using the gym that opened over on their side of town, no doubt. It doesn't match his try-hard nerdy look. Broad neck above a t-shirt with a logo I can't make out. His thick glasses have a brand name down one arm. It's all for show. He's not even that bright.

They're relocating for his new job, Rowena explained on the phone after I'd contacted her on Facebook about the cats, but I remember Ben switching course twice before he left university for good. In the damp kitchen in our shared house, Rowena sobbed over what she'd called the personality clash he'd had with his personal tutor.

"It's ever so lovely," she tries again. "Such pretty glass in the doors."

"Thank you," I say, still standing, and she fills us in on the progress of their packing. She'd never have guessed they have so much stuff.

"You have, you mean," Ben says. "Half of it's shoes and handbags."

She doesn't have anything to say to that. She's draped both their coats over the back of her armchair. Her lipstick is bright and she's left her scarf on. Polka dots cover her dress. Her hair is tied back and she must've got contacts. I don't imagine she's ever had the money for surgery.

Gym membership is expensive. I shouldn't think like that. They're obviously very happy. She made her choices and I made mine.

I'm sure I've seen that coat of hers. Ten years later and she hasn't bought a new one. No, I really mustn't think like that. Maybe she has others packed up ready to go down south. She's left her boots by the front door. I knew she would. It's easy to remember why I liked her so much.

"We'll let them out in a minute," she says to us all, watching the carry cases as though they might make a break for it on their own.

I step over them with exaggerated care—Celeste and I will be good at this, I want them to think—and take the gift bag and flowers into the kitchen, feeling an unreasonable pressure to get the flowers into water and the kettle on. This is what it's like to have ordinary guests, I remind myself.

"Just tea for us," Ben calls through.

"Please," Rowena adds.

The gift bag clunks onto the worktop. None of us are drinking so I won't open it. They've got an early start tomorrow and we're expecting our other guest later. I fuss around with four mugs, although we've only just had one, what with the waiting. I rinse Celeste's, but I left mine upstairs.

The tap gushes and splashes and I wish Rowena had come in here with me. I never stopped thinking about you, I want to tell her. All the things we shared when we lived in that dreadful house with the other girls. I didn't forget what she went through, but we can't talk about any of it tonight. It's hardly something I can communicate across the room with eye contact. She's covered it all up with that lipstick anyway, hidden it under that scarf. Did she ever even tell Ben?

The flowers go in the sink; I'll find a vase later. I don't want to miss anything, I tell myself. *You're anxious to supervise, that's just like you*, Celeste's voice says in my head. It sounds like her when she's nasty.

When I get back, I stop to take in the scene. The room is warm; the light is angled on everyone, the books are in shadow and so is the bed. That bed is the last thing Celeste and I want anyone to focus on. I go to draw the curtains, which I should've done earlier. Celeste says she feels like she's on stage if they're open after dark.

Celeste

"They'll be alright now," Ben says, glancing at the digital display on his watch. A few years ago, it would have had a calculator too. Rowena doesn't look sure, but he kneels down and undoes the doors.

One shoots under the sofa, the other winds around Rowena's legs as if it's casting a spell.

"So where did they come from?" Celeste asks, and I'm grateful to her for making conversation. Apart from the girls who come at night, we're not used to visitors and I wasn't sure we knew how to do this.

Rowena says, "From a rescue centre. It was Nancy we fell for. Such a sweetheart." She rubs the cat's chin with one finger. "The staff told us they were brother and sister and couldn't be separated."

Nancy is thin, wiry. It could be difficult not to prefer her, but maybe I'm drawn to the harder to help. I'm here with Celeste, aren't I? I shouldn't think like that. Nancy lifts her front paws off the carpet to bump her head against Rowena's hand.

"So they get on alright?" I ask doubtfully, turning my attention to Sid's tail sticking out from under the sofa as if he's forgotten it.

This is supposed to be temporary but we didn't discuss an end date. After their rough start, it might be better if the cats stay with us for a while. They couldn't possibly live in a flat. I'm looking forward to matching black circles on my quilt, wondering if we can put a flap in the back door. Nancy jumps onto the arm of the sofa next to Ben and sits with her eyes closed.

"Sort of," Rowena admits, making quick eye contact with Ben. She didn't tell me that on the phone. Did she say much about Sid at all? His tail flicks against the carpet.

"I reckon half the time they're not even related and they're just trying to get rid of them," Ben chips in. "Pretty sure I saw a ginger tom in with a rabbit."

We all laugh. Ben isn't so bad. I look over at Celeste, she's laughing too and not thinking about what's to come later. I'm so glad we offered to do this for Rowena, I'm so glad they came.

Three

"What are you in for?" Celeste asked.

We were alone in the waiting room. The other woman's name had been called. Relieved to get away from us, most likely. The receptionist had left too with a clipboard, probably feeling the same way. I should've known my appointment would be delayed.

"Sorry? In for?" My voice hadn't lost its shake, although my politeness had become more fragile.

She gestured around the room. A flash of those broad fingers. She showed me the blinds at the windows. A dozen empty chairs. Someone had picked the foam from the corner of one, I remember.

"Oh, that." I rolled up my sleeve, although the answer was all over my face. On one eyelid, down the furrow above my lip and creeping around my nostrils. "Vitiligo."

"Never heard of it." There was dismissiveness in her voice that made me feel I had to provide more compelling evidence.

"There isn't enough melanin in my skin. It makes these white patches."

"Oh. Will it get better?"

"Maybe. There's a new light therapy treatment. I've come to be assessed for a trial."

She ran a finger down my bare arm, stopping at the inside of my wrist and tapping it. "And that will work?"

"I don't know. It's a trial."

"Me, I'm here for my eczema." She scratched her thigh although she didn't seem to be reinforcing her point.

"Is it very bad, your eczema?"

"Celeste Harris? That's me, more or less," she announced, standing up. "They've never once got it right in here."

I blinked and remembered where we were.

The dermatologist stood in the doorway with a clipboard of her own. Celeste left her bag on the chairs and didn't ask me to watch it.

Alone with the ticking clock, I dared myself to look through that bag, but the temptation didn't come. There could be nothing to surprise me in there, nothing I didn't already know.

Four

"Got a girl coming tonight, then?" Rowena asks, and leans back against their coats and sips her tea.

They know about the girls. About the service we offer. I can only guess she doesn't disapprove. She's making conversation because she's a good guest. On the phone we laughed at how unalike we are, congratulated ourselves on supporting each other's choices, certain that's what they are.

"Is it right to call them girls?" Ben asks before either of us can answer, jokily hunkering down on the sofa as if protecting himself from a blow. "Shouldn't it be ladies? How old are they?"

"That's true," Rowena says, looking at him admiringly in a way I can't stand, as if he's thought of something she couldn't possibly have thought of herself.

"Well," I start, "most of them are—"

"Word crimes," Celeste interrupts, with a finger jabbed unfairly at Rowena, "you're all obsessed with them." Why can't she behave for one evening? These are my friends. Word crimes are an idea she probably picked up from one of those books I haven't read. For all I know, it'll be a chapter in the next one she wants to write too. "So busy monitoring each other's language you don't make a scrap of real difference."

Rowena's knuckles are tight against the handle of her mug and she pulls her legs closer to herself. Ben crosses his own and juts out that ugly chin. He thinks he's started Celeste off on something but he's too stupid to realise she isn't even prepared to argue on his terms. She's dismissed his whole premise. She could argue with him all night long but there's nothing in it for her.

"Yes, we do have someone coming later," I tell them over whatever Ben might've said next. "She's due in an hour or so. We don't know much about her."

"An hour?" Rowena asks, hurt. "We'd better not keep you."

They were late and I haven't seen them for ten years, but I don't say anything.

"Still," Ben pushes, "I expect some of them are very young, aren't they? Seventeen? Sixteen? Barely out of school, some of them. If that. You have to wonder what their lives are like. What they got themselves into to want to come to you."

And now our living room isn't so warm. The glass in the doors isn't even that pretty. I might as well blow out the candles and put on the main light. He's broken the magic.

Rowena touches her fist to her lips. "I don't know, of course, but I expect you never know who's going to come through the door, do you?" She's diplomatic, hedging, apologetic to her bones. I've tried to shake that off over the years and I don't like to see it in her.

Celeste smiles but it's forced. "They're girls or they're women and it doesn't matter what brings them here. It only matters what we can do for them."

Early on, Celeste looked at me that way too. She didn't like me to guess what brought the girls to us. It was hard. It still is. The last girl was sixteen but looked much younger. I've learned not to say anything like that to Celeste.

Ben doesn't want to talk about the girls anymore. It's too awkward and he wasn't that interested anyway. It turns out he's starting a company that delivers Friday night date kits to people's desks at work. A friend down south has developed an app.

"Couldn't he have developed an app that helps people?" Celeste asks, catching my eye. At least she didn't snort her tea.

"Oh, it does help people. No one has any time anymore." He launches into a speech that sounds like the presentation he might've made to his bank manager. "We funded it all online," he finishes, and I realise I was wrong.

Rowena handed in her notice at the Legal Aid department she loved, but she brushes that off and says their flat has a great view of the river.

She's not doing what she wants, that's for sure. She's waiting, life on hold, which isn't how she put it on the phone. When she's finished describing the boats that pass their dual aspect living space, she asks Celeste about her work, whether she's still at the university.

"I don't teach anymore," Celeste tells her. Her face is so red. I wish she'd move away from the fire. "They've invited me back as a fellow. My books are still on the reading list." Her smile is relaxed now. This is how I like to see her, thank God for Rowena.

"A *fellow*?" Ben says, that smirk on his face again. People probably tell him he's cheeky.

"It means she speaks to students from time to time, perhaps writes articles for journals, that sort of thing," Rowena explains, either not understanding what he meant or trying to hide it from us because he's such an embarrassment. She turns back to Celeste and asks about the students.

I don't hear the answer because Ben wants to know what I'm doing at the moment, although surely Rowena told him.

"I'm having a break from work." There isn't anywhere he can take that and I won't help him out, so conversation turns to television, presumably safer than anyone's career or unaccompanied teenagers coming to women like us.

Fortunately, we've all been watching Nordic crime dramas. "It rains so much!" I say, and Ben explains in some detail how the weather adds to the moodiness. We all nod along while he does this, even Celeste.

"I'm sorry but I have to say this," Rowena starts when he's finished. She's hesitant, choosing her words. She frowns as if she's weighing it up, putting forward her argument the way I remember her in seminars. She used to shuffle and shunt a dozen cue cards on the table in front of her, ever-prepared, ever-Rowena. "I'm sorry but I wonder if we shouldn't be asking questions about the gender of the victims in these series. It seems they're often young girls."

Ben stands up to examine a wooden toadstool on the mantelpiece. I bought it for Celeste from a National Trust stately home five or six years ago. I'm surprised he finds it so fascinating.

"That's an interesting point," I say to Rowena. Ben puts the toadstool back and it topples over. "Do you think they reflect reality, or is it cheap sensationalism to keep viewers watching?" Celeste lets her blanket fall and turns to Rowena to hear what she'll say.

Rowena is pleased to be asked. She and Ben probably haven't got past talking about what the weather might bring. "Well–"

"The women over there, they really let themselves go," he interrupts from the middle of the room, blocking all our light. He didn't stand Celeste's toadstool up. "They get to a certain age then hack their hair off, no make-up, these horrible baggy clothes." He swallows the last of his tea, and puts his mug on the carpet next to the empty carry cases. "Anyway, better take a leak before we set off."

He leaves, following my directions, and Rowena sighs. "I'd love to go."

"Sorry?" I say, thinking she means the bathroom too.

"Oh, you know. Go. Like those women. Let go of all this." She looks down at herself and gestures with floppy wrists. She means the dress, the lipstick, the scarf.

There's nothing we can say to that. Celeste is wearing one of my old headscarves, pulled over her forehead, almost down to her eyes. I saw the looks they gave it when they came in. I wanted to tell them it wasn't a pair of underpants, but couldn't make myself say the words in case they didn't laugh.

Rowena picks up Ben's mug and takes all four to the kitchen. There's that easy way about her again, knowing the right thing to do. Normal just comes to her. The flowers and wine were her idea, there's no way Ben would've thought of that.

I follow her. It's cold in here because I opened the window after I cooked the chilli. Wetness still streaks down the cupboard fronts.

"Are you alright?" I ask her, knowing the question is too big.

She rinses our mugs, twisting the tap away from the flowers. "Yes," she says, and pretends something has attracted her attention out there in the dark garden. "I'll miss them, of course." She means the cats.

"But how are you *really*?"

"Fine," she says brightly, all smiles. "Excited about the big move."

Of course this isn't the time. Celeste and Ben are through there, and this isn't the kitchen in the student house. This is the future we worried about then and there's no room for the past in here.

"I'm sorry we haven't been in touch for so long," I say. "If only we lived closer!"

She smiles at my joke. We're less than three miles apart, but we both know our lives have got in the way. No wonder she seemed embarrassed and surprised on the phone, but it's my fault too, of course, and I want her to know that. "Let's not leave it so long next time," she says, taking my hand and squeezing my fingers.

It occurs to me sadly as we go back through that she might be pregnant, and I wonder what she'll do.

Celeste

Ben reappears, wiping his hands on his jeans to show us he washed them. He moves around as if he's gathering up their belongings but there's only their coats on the back of the chair.

They stroke Nancy where she's balancing on the armrest and Rowena whispers something to her. Neither of them tries to coax Sid out.

I close the front door behind them and watch their blurry shapes through the mottled glass. The last I see is Rowena's bright scarf going around to the driver's side because Ben says he's too tired.

When I get back to the living room, it's sad and comforting to see the mess they've left us. The floor is hidden under bags of food, the carry cases and the litter trays. I help Celeste up and we stand back to assess our arrivals, one just a tail.

"Where do you think they'll sleep?" I ask.

"Wherever they want. I don't think we're getting him out from under there tonight. But I do know one thing."

"What's that?"

"We'll have to change their names."

Five

"What did Dr Ali say? Will you have the light therapy?"

"I have to ring for a follow-up in a fortnight. First of eight sessions."

She'd waited for me, reading a book she must've had in her bag. "You should come home with me," she said bluntly, the way I hadn't been asked before. She didn't say anything else until we were outside. She didn't do anything to reinforce the point either. She never did.

In the car park, she told me her flat was twenty minutes from the hospital. Her bag went on the backseat and her hand went on my leg. It's no use pretending she didn't feel the shake.

Ten minutes later, we were up the stairs and at her front door. There were holiday photos on the wall in her hallway. A younger Celeste and a dark-haired woman in sunglasses. I wondered if I should care whether that woman still came up those stairs or through that front door.

Celeste's bag went on her bedroom floor and I went in her bed. She told me my skin was a map of another world, which I'd heard women say before, although never one like her. "I can trace islands. Cross borders. Discover continents." I wasn't so young I didn't know it was flattery but I was already in her bed.

I whispered to the ceiling, "The other children. Swimming lessons. The teacher told me I couldn't go in wearing my leotard. She thought we couldn't afford anything else and took scissors to the sleeves."

She kissed my stomach. "Oceans on another planet."

"And where are you going now?" I was too caught up to care I'd laid another trap for myself.

"South," she said. It was clumsy and corny, but I didn't ring Dr Ali for a follow-up appointment.

Six

As soon as Rowena and Ben left, Celeste went to open the window in the guest bedroom. Her arthritis slows her on the stairs but she's obsessed with airing things out. By the time I've lugged the sacks of cat food into the kitchen and emptied the dishwasher, she's sitting on the single bed in my dressing gown and a strong breeze.

"It's freezing in here," I say. "There's fog in the forecast overnight. It only smells of chilli anyway. This girl's not going to complain, is she?" I close the window and draw the curtains, and throw a clump of hair from the duvet cover into the bin.

"It needed the air. The fog won't *get in*, if that's what you're afraid of."

"No, it's not that—"

"You think it'll choke us in our sleep, wrap its ghostly fingers round our necks," she teases. She reaches for me, her hands on my waist.

I put my hands over hers. Her skin's cold and dry. "I don't."

I wish those were the things I'm afraid of, not the way she coughs after breakfast. She goes out into the garden and pretends to be checking on things but really she's gasping for air. It's worse in the mornings, she tells me, that's all. And in the evenings.

She was well again today, I think when we let go. Is that four days in a row? It only makes me wonder how long it's been since that last happened. Six weeks? She stands up and shrugs off my dressing gown. I put it on. My hand closes around a balled-up tissue in the pocket.

"I like the smell of you," she says, as if it needs an explanation. It's the comfort she wants, it's not about sex.

I move the towels from the bed to the dressing table. There's a separate one for their hair, and a flannel they don't usually use. There's a bar of soap in its wrapper on top of the pile too, and we save the shampoo samples that come through the door. We're going for practical but not clinical. Homely but not home. The telephone rang three days ago.

"We should've re-done this room," Celeste says, standing in the doorway, shrunken in her ordinary clothes. "Too late now." She's right. We both know this girl will be our last.

Celeste didn't understand the things I wanted for this house, the changes I wanted to make. She argued for a new build—orange brick and white window frames, small children in helmets, unsteady on their bikes in the street—but she let me win in the end. I like the creaks and the condensation, the grooves and the gaps.

"People don't like brown furniture, Emma," she declares like it's a fact. "They throw it out, repaint it, anything. It's heavy, it's dark and it's depressing."

"It's retro," I explain yet again.

"It's old."

"You are retro. So be grateful I like old stuff." I didn't used to tease her and I regret it this time. She bows her head, humiliated.

She shakes it off and moves to smack my arse but stops herself. The mood isn't right in here.

"I might as well go to bed, then. Good night," she says, but she doesn't leave.

Perhaps she wants to talk about it. It feels good to focus on the mundane, the detail. It could fool any of us into thinking we've got control. Celeste might say that's me trying to oversee everything, but I don't think so.

"She'll have got on a flight after work. Not the ferry, this time. They told me on the phone. She'll get a taxi here and another one tomorrow morning. They gave her a name to use."

No one can know she's here. She'll be arrested and that's a life sentence. I don't know if it's the same if they're very young. The idea is too dramatic for Celeste these days, I can't ask her. This girl is staying the night before, but most stay the night afterwards.

I walk around the room so Celeste can watch me. There must be something else I can do in here, something I can move or rearrange.

"This is probably the worst thing ever to happen to her," I say, putting a packet of sanitary towels into the bottom of the empty wardrobe. Three wire hangers rattle into one another as I close the door.

Celeste

"Let's hope so," Celeste says. "For the love of God, let's hope so."

Seven

I knew it was wrong before I opened the door, but it was too late to change my mind. It was the only pub on the street.

"Arrow and Bluebird? Don't think I've been in this one," Celeste remarked, her arm in mine. I caught sight of her hard-to-impress reflection in the door's glass as it swung.

It was our first proper date, in a city centre pub I'd wanted to try for a while. I was still dressed for the office. I was only a couple of weeks into the administration job I'd taken that had nothing to do with my degree. I'd planned to leave the city after graduation—more opportunities in my field back home, but then I'd met Celeste. She might've at least washed her fleece.

Every man in the place had a strongman beard, whether staff or patron. The girls were all tattooed. It was fashionable and ridiculous and I should've known better. Celeste went to find a table and I stood at the bar and hoped our drinks would be served in something ordinary.

When I turned to watch her go, no one else was looking at her. There wasn't the wowed silence she deserved. They only saw a shapeless elderly woman with untamed hair.

There was some hold-up at the bar and they'd bring our drinks to us.

"These are the two I wrote," she told me when I returned to her, slapping two paperbacks onto the table. I realised I hadn't a clue what else might be in that bag. "You can have them, if you like."

I pulled them towards me and spun them the right way round in turn with one finger. "Women's Studies? That's what you teach?" No wonder I'd never seen her on the campus. My faculty had been nowhere near hers.

"Yes. Although most HE institutions call it Gender Studies now."

From her tone, I knew she disapproved of that. I waited for her to continue her point, provide some supporting evidence, but she didn't. The covers gave nothing away. "So what are they about?"

She looked past me, bored. I wasn't enough. Soon she'd find someone else the way she found me. She could have anyone she wanted, anywhere but here. Imagine picking a girl up in a hospital waiting room.

"Oh, this and that," she said, unhelpfully. A girl carried drinks on a tray to a table nearby. Celeste watched her go, her desire so obvious. Doors to the kitchen slammed and someone started up a video game machine.

My insides reeled and heaved. I could lose Celeste if I didn't say something. When the idea came to me I couldn't think of a thing wrong with it. Not even its vagueness put me off.

"I want to *do* something," I said. Once that was out, she leant towards me, forearms on the table and bottom on the edge of her chair. I might have said something like, "I've always wanted to *do* something. To help people somewhere. I've been worried to go abroad because of my skin. I have to avoid the sun, you see." Was I still thinking about that then? I must have been. I was still so young, so interested in myself.

"You should do something for women," Celeste said. "Loving women is the most radical thing you can do in this world." I didn't know then she was paraphrasing someone else.

I lied in a hurry. "Right. Yes. That's what I was thinking."

She was patient while I explained that I knew environmental disasters and climate change hit women harder than men. "Women and girls aren't taught to swim so they're much more likely to drown in floods, and they're less well-fed so they don't cope so well with famine or disease. They're vulnerable to sexual assault in refugee camps, lack adequate facilities to cope with their periods…"

She wasn't listening, she knew all that already. She was just watching me talk. I wanted her to take me seriously so I pressed on, making a foolish grand statement about not expecting to see change in my lifetime. "Even some feminists here are unwilling to share their spaces with trans women–"

That she interrupted. "Hold on. Trans women? What makes them women? Because they like wearing mascara and skirts?" So she had been listening.

We were wearing neither but she was intent on riling me, my punishment for choosing the wrong pub or for not asking the right questions about her books. "Oh, come on. They feel like women inside."

"And how exactly does it feel to feel like a woman inside, Emma? How could a man know?"

I couldn't answer. I hated her refusal to just accept.

"You're destroying the movement by letting men in," she said, taking her books back as if I personally was to blame. "Years ago we wouldn't have believed it would end up like this. What I wouldn't give to–"

"Go back in time. Yes, I know. You said that when we met."

"Brain sex has been debunked. Gender is a hoax," she said, in a way that told me she'd said it often. "We are oppressed by men because of our sex. Our biology. So you should put actual women first in whatever you do." She sat back as if that put an end to it. She used her age to her advantage and there was nothing I could say. Her and her sodding books. If only I'd known to accuse her of *word crimes* then.

"But we don't agree who qualifies as actual women," I said, stupidly taking the last word.

She said nothing when our drinks arrived in jam jars.

* * *

"I've got a special birthday coming up," she told me when we were walking back to her flat, arms by our sides.

Fifty-five? Sixty at most, I was sure. "Hmmm," I said, stung by our argument and not in the mood to indulge her.

"I'll be seventy," she said.

I almost stopped mid-step, but said nothing of my surprise. "You should have your friends over. Who was it sent that lovely Christmas card you left up? Jo and Sarah? You said you'd like to see them again. Invite them."

"Oh, I can't be bothered with all that."

She exasperated me. I was certain she'd never want me to meet them. I wasn't enough. "What *would* you like?" I knew her answer the moment I finished the question.

"Move in with me and we'll do your thing together."

Eight

I'm still in my clothes under my dressing gown. I've been eating crisps and flicking through a magazine site on my tablet, not wanting to miss the knock on the door. The radiators up here are off so I don't fall asleep. It's impossible to concentrate on an article telling me how to wow at the office Christmas party because every sound might be the girl's arrival. I hear Celeste sneeze comically loudly downstairs and hope she isn't allergic to the cats. I don't know what we'll do with them if she is. All these years later, that eczema hasn't cleared up either.

Celeste is in bed down there. We had to get rid of one of the sofas to make room for it, but this evening we could've forgotten it's there. Rowena and Ben probably didn't even notice. It's not electric, Celeste wouldn't hear of that. She bought it from a local supplier, a family-run business. The brand name reassured and pleased her although I'd never heard of it.

She's dying, of course. We both know that. She's facing those little indignities before the final injustice. She's frequently grumpy and always in pain. She's not a perfect patient; a liar when I ask her how she feels and a whiner when I'm occupied with anything but her.

"Cancer of the breast," she announced to me sharply one afternoon when she returned from an appointment she hadn't told me about. She's undergoing treatment but it feels like a sop for me, and it hasn't stopped the spread.

It's raining now. I hear it shaking through the leaves on the tree outside. I go over to look out, and here's my empty mug on the window sill again, cold against my hand. We need to do something about the bird table in the front garden. The squirrels get at it, but Celeste doesn't mind. They're all the same to her, all in need. The street beyond our garden is dark and quiet. I look at my reflection in the glass. Could I really have been any woman in any life, if I'd chosen it? There's no sign of the girl's taxi yet.

I cross the room back to my tablet and settle cross-legged in the dip on my quilt. The magazine isn't enough to keep me from typing Celeste's illness into the browser again. I've visited every site on the first three pages of results, most of them more than once. I click and scroll with my fingertip until I find something new.

Everything on the page blurs and I'm convinced she has it all and it's hopeless. We shouldn't have moved here, she was right. A new build on a housing estate would've been better. This room, this house, it's pretty but there's no one for me to talk to here. There are plenty Celeste's age, like Alan with the dog next door, but she refuses. If that's my punishment for wanting this house, it's a cruel one.

Having the girls stay makes me wonder if I was wrong, maybe Celeste is always making a point. She was so quick to agree to it. Her voice in my head says scornfully, *They don't come to us because of their gender, Emma.*

There's a quick, quiet knock. I take the stairs carefully. When I open the door I light a rectangle of rain on the front step. She must be used to this weather, I think, because I can't help myself. She hasn't got the usual pull-along suitcase.

"Hello," I whisper, and stand back to let her in. "I'm Emma."

"Sophie." I'm surprised by her accent, the way I always am. She has a vintage holdall I think about complimenting. This doesn't get any easier. There's something in her hair, a soggy fabric flower, and she has an umbrella she doesn't struggle with. Her taxi pulls away, its headlights swinging over the slick road.

I take her coat. She's wearing a cardigan and a jumper underneath. Her shirt has a pussy-bow collar and her hair spills out of a messy bun. Everything is slipping off her, but that's the fashion. She pulls her boots off and steps onto the hall tiles in her tights. She's shivering.

"Can I get you a drink?" I ask.

"Please. Tea?" She pronounces it *tae*.

"Of course."

I show her into the guest bedroom upstairs, our voices low so we don't disturb Celeste.

She puts her holdall on the bed and tells me she got herself into a bit of a state on the plane. "The man across the aisle was nice, dead-on, but I wanted to close my eyes."

"How do you feel now?"

"Fine. Tired. I didn't sleep last night for worry. I'm so ascared my ma will find out."

I've heard this story before and I haven't heard it at all. "Where does your ma think you are now?"

"Staying with my sister. I told her I was coming here. She won't say anything."

"Good. It'll be alright." She looks at the wall behind me because we both know the truth. "What time's your appointment?"

"I have to be there by eight."

"I'll be up at six. Come and find me in the kitchen."

I tell her where the bathroom is, fetch her tea then go through to Celeste. There's a thumped pillow on the floor I have to step over. She's awake and propped up in bed, and the fire is low. I sit on the duvet next to Nancy, who I could believe has forgotten Rowena and Ben entirely. The clock on the mantelpiece says it's already morning.

"Your hands are freezing," Celeste complains, holding them against her cheek. "I heard the knock. I hope you've left her on her own to get on with things. What's this one like?"

"Very millennial."

"What's that?"

I don't tell her they've been screwed over by her generation, although part of me would like revenge for the way she blames me for mine.

"I just mean she's young. On another day, she'd be in a tiger onesie, photographing her lunch on her phone. Half of them that age have given up any hope of adulthood."

"Young like you?" There are long strands of her hair all over the pillow. I'm forever vacuuming or shaking something out these days.

My voice rises and my jaw tightens despite myself. I take my hand from her cheek. "No, not like me. Ten years younger than me. Fifteen years, maybe."

"As young as that?" she says shaking her head, as if anyone could be so young.

"Yes." And they come here, to go through this with us.

Nine

Celeste leant against the worktop with the back door open. The removal men were unwrapping an unframed canvas in the living room and I almost staggered into them.

"Where do you want these, Celeste?" I called.

"Wherever you want."

That meant I was supposed to know already. My back hurt, I'd been lifting boxes all day and I wasn't in the mood to guess.

Celeste's city centre flat had shot up in value and her father had died in a care home somewhere on the south coast. She'd never mentioned him when he was alive and I hadn't asked. I was still so caught up in myself, although at least I wasn't so preoccupied with my skin.

She'd probably want her books in the living room, I decided. I put them down and stretched my back with my hands on the base of my spine. She came through to hand me a cup of tea. "You know, I thought I'd been cut out of the will," she said. "Dad read the articles about my first book after it was published. I was always too strident for him." She laughed. "Staunch. Militant."

"But he must've loved you?"

"He'd rather have died than seen a penny of his go to the dogs' home."

That made me laugh too. One of the removal men looked on, trying to work us out.

"'Over my dead body,' he said," Celeste added, milking it. She rinsed her mug and I wrapped my hands around my own as if I was unwell.

We went outside and she picked up a stick from the lawn that must've blown over from next door's tree. I ran down the path like a child so she could see how pleased everything had made me.

I called over my shoulder, "We could keep chickens at the bottom of the garden, there's space for a coop, look. It'd be perfect."

"Oh, but what about foxes? I couldn't bear it." Her hands were on her lips, more sentimental than I'd ever seen her.

Celeste

"What about a bird feeder on that lovely tree round the front then? Or a bird table?"

"Good idea," she said, and walked towards me, hardy and lumbering. The garden became where I liked to watch her move.

Her jeans were torn to bits, long past the point of fashion. They gaped and bagged around her knees. "You need another pair of those," I said.

"No point now, is there?" My cheerfulness vanished in the dust of her remark.

"It's not too late to do something, is it?" I whispered to her later that night, her arm around my shoulders in bed, soil under our fingernails.

"Of course not. Silly." She pulled her arm from under me, lifted herself onto one elbow, and looked down. "We'll do your thing. Do you know what you want to do yet?"

"I think so." I stretched and took hold of her hand above my head. "I need to make a couple of phone calls tomorrow." I listened to her breathing and looked up at the unfamiliar ceiling. I saw a face in the beam I lost a moment later. It felt right to ask the question I always wanted to ask. "What will I do after you've gone?"

She let go and turned to face the wall. I put my arm around her waist, hoping she'd come back to me. She didn't. She'd never talk about what would happen next. For her it was as though we were living at the end of something. The time worth having was already wasting away.

My God, I thought, as I clung to her. *We almost missed each other.*

Less than a month later, our first arrival came to us. The clinic assured me we weren't too far away. I took extra blankets in that night and thought about lighting a candle, but she might've seen some significance in it.

Ten

Last night's mugs are upside-down on the draining board where Rowena left them. I'll put them in the dishwasher later. I take three more from the cupboard while the kettle hisses and steams. Water runs down the window pane and pools on the tiles behind the sink. I pull out a box of herbal and a jar of instant although we don't touch either ourselves.

Sid is licking his front paw on top of the fridge. When I take out the milk, he hunches down to watch me. I'm careful to ignore him. Celeste hasn't come in from the living room. This won't be a fifth good day.

Sophie is sitting at the kitchen table, stunned and polite.

"Here you go," I say, putting a box of cereal in front of her. I'm trying not to hover, Celeste would tell me to back off, but this girl has to eat, doesn't she?

"Thank you," she says. "Thank you for having me here. I had to save in such a hurry to come. It's a good job I've got, so it is. I could send you money in a few months."

I open my mouth to refuse, my hand is up, ready to wave her offer away. It's what Celeste has always done. But what about the next girl? We could send it on to the clinic. There must be a scheme.

"You don't have to do that," I say, anyway.

The abortion costs them hundreds of pounds, then there's the flight over here. Some come on the ferry because it's cheaper and if they don't have a place to stay, they'll bleed into the seats on their way home. It takes them so long to save up, and the price rises with every passing week.

"I'm with the baby's father," she says, and I'm about to wave this confidence away too. Like the money, we're not here for that. But she wants to tell me, or thinks she should. "There's something wrong with it. It won't survive. I can't carry on, knowing that."

"I understand," I say, because there isn't anything else.

It smells unhealthy in the living room, like unwashed bedding and leftover food. If only it weren't November, I'd open the window.

"So this will be the last one?" Celeste asks when I get in bed next to her. She knows it will. We can't cope anymore. We have to turn in on ourselves. "How many did we have altogether?"

"Nineteen, I think, including this one."

"Which one was first? Remind me."

Sophie walks past the glass in the living room door and sees us.

I snuggle closer. Our visitor will use the bathroom and I don't want to go upstairs. She doesn't need to hear me banging about. That's what Celeste would say. "The first one was a student and didn't want to leave her course."

Celeste leans back to look at my face. "No, that's not right. She was older, the first one, I'm sure. Wasn't she a doctor herself?"

I prepare to tell the story and part of Celeste stays in the bed with me, listening. But while she listens, it's as if another part of her was there back then, alongside me. Celeste is there when I found Rowena white-faced in the kitchen, the day we were due to go home after our first term. We'd decorated the house for Christmas even though none of us had planned to stay.

"We were drunk," Rowena explained, blindly stuffing takeaway cartons into a black plastic sack next to the overflowing bin. A cheap string of fairy lights clattered down the back of the fridge as she shouldered into it.

I looked for rubber gloves in the cupboard under the sink, the kindest thing I could think to do. "It'll be okay," I told her. I didn't know for sure, but it had to be, didn't it? There'd be a doctor's appointment—Rowena was probably the only one amongst us to have registered with a local GP—and then it'd be taken care of. "I'll come with you."

"My train's at 14:03," she said, precise under pressure, the way she always was. "I can't go home. They'll see it on my face. Everyone will be there for Christmas. Oh God, Emma, I can't wait until the New Year. I can't."

We walked to the surgery along the canal bank, the grass either side of the tow path heavy and silver with frost. "I can't believe I left it this long, but I didn't realise we'd slept together until the morning after," she said, eyes showing above her winter scarf. "I was so drunk he offered to bring me home and look after me, since he hadn't had that much himself."

Celeste is right there behind me on the path, it seems to me, in the corner of my eye. In my story, I say to Rowena, "So you don't remember saying yes?"

A woman in a knitted hat and a long coat stood back to let us pass. "Funny you remember that," Celeste observes, beside me in bed.

"I'd bought the same hat for my mother that Christmas," I tell her.

"Oh. I liked how you described the frost on the grass too. Atmospheric. Good you're finally putting your degree to use."

"So you don't remember saying yes?" I repeat, to get back to what happened.

Rowena said, "Well… no. But it was my fault. Poor Ben, what was he supposed to think?"

I tell Celeste, "We made up a story so our parents wouldn't find out. I can't remember what we said, probably that we had freshers' flu and couldn't face the train. Rowena said Ben was so wrapped up, struggling with his essays, constantly missing deadlines and arranging meetings with his tutors. He was under so much pressure, she said."

Celeste is quiet for a moment. "And you didn't say anything to anybody?"

"I thought we could deal with it ourselves and it'd be over. We'd start the next term as if nothing had happened."

"And how did that go?"

I shift myself and pull the duvet off my legs. I hadn't expected her to ask that. "Fine. Well, I think so. Rowena didn't mention it again. She moved out and went to live with some other friends from her course the next term."

"So Rowena was the first girl?"

I nod, suddenly tearful, thinking about Rowena leaving with Ben last night.

"You said Rowena seemed surprised to hear from you."

It's now I realise I belong to a part of Rowena's life she'd rather forget. She wasn't surprised to hear from me because our lives had grown apart, but because of what she'd been through with me.

Celeste

"I'm away now," the girl calls from the hall.

"Coming," I say and scramble out from under the tangle of sheets and blankets.

I watch her get into the taxi from the doorstep. Last night's rain has littered the front lawn with orange leaves. She'll have something rehearsed for the driver. They'll enjoy each other's accents, make a joke of it and the journey will be that much quicker. When she gets off the plane tonight, she'll have to have something better prepared for her family. Her steps will slow and her heart will race. Should I assume she's never done this before?

For those who make it here and back, there'll be months of jumping at every knock on the door, every time the phone rings. They'll search their mothers' faces for knowing, never sure whether they once made this trip too, never able to say. Sisters, cousins, friends, secrets hung onto for a lifetime. Her taxi pulls out and makes its way over the speedbumps and around the corner.

Upstairs, I find sixty pounds on my fifties dressing table.

I go to tell Celeste. She has the television on with the sound down. We'll have the fire lit again today. Make it a different room for the daytime.

"She wouldn't want to have been caught with English money and have to explain it," Celeste says. "They use Irish pounds over there. It's different." She's trying to educate me still.

"Euros," I say gently. "They use Euros now. They have done for years."

She grunts and turns the television up. Nancy stretches her front legs and pushes her claws into the blanket.

"I'll make breakfast," I say. "Toast?"

Celeste makes an agreeing sort of noise, and I kiss her head. She waves at me to move out of the way of the television. I open the kitchen door and Sid slips past my legs. The sun is up now, hazy through the clouds. From the window, I see a plane passing overhead. I grip the edge of the worktop and watch it go. For a moment, I don't think I can do it. I am certain I can't turn around and make breakfast for Celeste. I can't carry on.

The plane disappears into a cloud and I turn on the tap to fill the kettle. There is bread to put in the toaster and butter in the fridge.

Celeste

As I sit Celeste up and balance the tray on her lap, I wonder if the girl will think of us one day when the skies clear, remembering a night in a pretty house with two women. One of them is probably dead now, she'll think, rationality mixed with a fondness she can't quite account for. Were they sisters? She'll never know. The older one slept in a bed downstairs and she didn't really speak to her. Funny English women, there won't be anyone like that now, doing what they did. How terrible such a thing was ever needed.

And I will sit in this room alone, in my future you'd never talk about. I'll sit and I'll think and I'll hope we did what we could. We did, though, didn't we, Celeste? Didn't we do what we could?

Practicing Self-Love by Priscilla Lugo

Practicing self-love is hard. It's a long, difficult and emotional process of convincing yourself that you are good enough, that you are beautiful enough, and that who you are as a person is just enough. It's especially hard when everywhere you look you're being told that who you are and what you look like don't fit into the conventional standards of beauty that were set before us. This is why self-love is arguably harder for Latinas because for the most part, we look like the complete opposite of the European beauty standards that plague our society.

Growing up, girls constantly see what is considered beautiful; they see it in commercials, television shows, movies, magazines, etc., and what they see isn't much different from one to another. All that is seen is fair skin, with light eyes and light hair. But when Latinas look in the mirror all that they see (for the most part) is brown skin, brown eyes, and brown hair. It seems as if brown is all you see, and from a young age we are taught that brown isn't beautiful. Products are marketed towards us in order to make us more conventionally beautiful. We are sold products like sun-in, skin-lightening products, as well as Nair and razors that take away our beautiful brown skin, hair, and our bodies. We are told to change everything that makes Latinas beautiful and unique.

Our brownness isn't the only thing that makes practicing self-love hard. Our bodies also play a part in the battle of self-love. When our bodies don't conform to the stereotypical Latina of being thick and curvy, we are often not seen as Latina enough. This is not only toxic in regards to self-love, but it can also lead to identity issues. What people fail to realize is that each Latina has a different set of experiences that shape how she sees herself, and that Latinas come in all shapes and sizes. Yet, we are often told that if we don't look like JLo or Sofia Vergara, we aren't beautiful Latinas.

Latinas, like all women of color, are constantly being told that if they don't fit into the European standards of beauty then they aren't beautiful. So naturally, it's hard to have a loving relationship with yourself and with your body when all your whole life you've been at war with it in attempts to conform to what society tells us is beautiful. But it's possible. It's possible to love yourself and your body as a Latina, and a WoC; the process is just so much longer and more difficult. You have to come to terms with not being accurately represented in the media, that you will always be different than what you see on television (and different isn't a bad thing), and that there will be times when you do want to change certain things about yourself, but that doesn't make you any less worthy of loving yourself.

Learning to love yourself is a long and strenuous battle that can take years to achieve, but it starts with you deciding that you are worthy, beautiful, and incredible even if you don't necessarily believe it at the time because soon enough you will. It's convincing yourself that even though it seems like everything is against you and your beauty, you are so extremely beautiful. You are a beautiful entity that doesn't and shouldn't need validation from others to recognize the true extent of your magnificent beauty. We are all so beautiful that it's practically blinding. We are all so worthy of self-love that it is overwhelming. Together we can dismantle the social norms by establishing a new status quo that everyone is beautiful. Don't accept anything less than what you deserve and remember, brown is beautiful, too.

Room For Our Courage

Prologue/Epilogue by Lorrie Hartshorn

She hears the whisper of the breeze and feels it on her bare arms a second later, cool in the comforting heat. Her eyelids, closed against the light, rest gentle as moths, her eyelashes long against the curve of her cheek.

Mottled shadows fall across her brow; sweat dampens her hairline just a little but she is comfortable. The aches and strains of another day fade, and she thinks about her son—her lovely son—who will be coming to visit her soon.

The hum of voices reaches her ears but doesn't disturb her; the blanket is soft beneath her body and it feels so good to rest, just for a moment. The low chime of a bell, far away, and the rustle of trees. She senses movement nearby but knows she is safe.

She lets sleep take her.

* * *

He hears the hiss of the ventilator and watches as the hairs on her bare arms rise as the air touches her a second later, cool in the suffocating heat of the ICU. Her eyelids, taped shut against the lights, rest gentle as moths, her eyelashes stuck with dried blood to the curve of her fractured cheek.

Mottled bruises leave an indigo trail across her brow; sweat beads at her hairline but she must be kept warm. The pain from the attack is numbed by diamorphine, and her son—her only son—has arrived to find her in hospital, as he always feared he would.

The hum of voices reaches them from the nurses' station but she doesn't move; the blanket beneath her body is crumpled and stained, and she's been sedated for now. The sudden chime of an alarm on the machine next to the bed, and uniforms appear, pushing and bustling by the bed, guiding him out of the room.

He lets them take him.

Your Silence Will Not Protect You: Racism in the Feminist Movement by Claire Heuchan

A brief foreword: This is the first in a series of blog posts on race and racism in the feminist movement. It is not a feel-good piece. Equally, it is not a reprimand. It is a wake-up call—one which I hope will be answered.

Solidarity between women is vital for liberation. If the feminist movement is to succeed, feminist principles must be applied in deed as well as in word. Although intersectionality is used as a buzzword in contemporary activism, in many ways we have deviated from Crenshaw's intended purpose: bringing marginalised voices from the periphery to the centre of the feminist movement by highlighting the coexistence of oppressions. White women with liberal politics routinely describe themselves as being intersectional feminists before proceeding to speak over and disregard those women negotiating marginalised identities of race, class, and sexuality in addition to sex. Intersectionality as virtue-signalling is diametrically opposed to intersectional praxis. The theory did not emerge in order to aid white women in their search for cookies—it was developed predominantly by Black feminists with a view to giving women of colour voice.

White feminists of all stripes are falling down at the intersection of race. Liberal feminists frequently fail to consider racism in terms of structural power. Radical feminists are often unwilling to apply the same principles of structural analysis to oppression rooted in race as in sex.

White women who are self-proclaimed feminists have a habit of expecting women of colour to choose between identities of race and sex, to prioritise challenging misogyny over opposing racism, in the name of sisterhood. Classic Black feminist texts dating from the early 1970s onwards detail this phenomenon, and precious little about interracial dynamics between women have changed since their publication. What white women often fail to consider is that, for women of colour, race and sex are inextricably linked in how we experience the world, how we are situated within structures of power. Yet discussion of race is often treated like a derailment from the Real Feminist Issues (i.e. those relating directly to white women), the implication being that women of colour are at most a sub-group within the movement.

Regardless of how their feminist politics manifest, the question of race is one that is not so easily answered, or even acknowledged, by many white women. Through both feminist theory and activism, women develop a structural understanding of the patriarchal hierarchy and where we are positioned within that system. Techniques such as consciousness raising and collective organisation have enabled women to connect the personal with the political—and it is deeply personal. Within feminism, women become fully aware of how we are marginalised by patriarchy. White women rightly consider themselves to belong to the oppressed class in terms of sex. Being aware of the implications carried by belonging to the dominant class, white women are therefore discomfited by the notion of being the oppressing party in the hierarchy of race (hooks, 2000). This brings us to our first fallacy:

'Making it about race divides women.'

Time and time again, this line is used by white women to circumnavigate any meaningful discussion of race, to avoid the discomfiting possibility of having to confront the spectre of their own racism. This argument suggests that the effort of feminist women would be best concentrated on challenging sex-based oppression at the exclusion of all other manifestations of prejudice. In adopting such a narrow approach to activism, such women preclude the possibility of tackling misogyny's root cause: white supremacist capitalist patriarchy (hooks, 1984).

Sole focus on misogyny is, ultimately, ineffective. Selective structural analysis will only take us so far. Racism and classism, like misogyny, are pillars of white supremacist capitalist patriarchy, upholding and perpetuating dominant power structures. Patriarchy cannot be dismantled whilst the other vectors in the matrix of domination (Hill Collins, 2000) remain in place. Such laissez-faire politics and activism lack the depth, rigour, and ethical consistency required to drive a cultural shift towards liberation. They also beg the question: what sort of feminism looks on, indifferent, when injustice thrives?

No, talking about race does not divide women. It is racism that does that—specifically, the racism white women direct towards women of colour, the racism that white women observe and fail to challenge because, ultimately, they benefit from it. Whether intentional or casually delivered, that racism has the same result: it completely undermines the possibility of solidarity between women of colour and white women. White women's unwillingness to explore the subject of race, to acknowledge the ways in which they benefit from white supremacy, makes mutual trust impossible.

'But white women don't benefit from white supremacy.'

To argue that misogyny is the primary agent in all women's oppression is to assume that the category of 'woman' overlaps entirely with 'white' and 'middle class', which plainly isn't the case. The hierarchy of race has as much bearing on the lived experiences of women of colour as the hierarchy of gender. When roughly 70% of British people in jobs paying the national minimum wage are women, it is evident that class plays a pivotal role in the lives of working class women.

Frequently white women complain about brocialism—the tendency of leftist men to remain mysteriously incapable of noticing how the hierarchy of social class is mirrored by that of gender. This is a valid critique, a necessary critique. It is also a critique that is entirely applicable to white, self-proclaimed feminist women unwilling to engage with anti-racist politics. Even as they experience classism and/or lesbophobia, white women continue to benefit from their whiteness.

According to the Fawcett Society, the gender pay gap for full-time employees sits at 13.9%. BAME (Black and Minority Ethnic) people with GCSEs are paid 11% less than our white counterparts, a deficit that rises to 23% among graduates. In addition, BAME graduates are more than twice as likely to be unemployed than white graduates. Women of colour face a double jeopardy of sorts, our labour undervalued both on grounds of race and sex. Zora Neale Hurston once described Black women as the "mule uh de world", an observation that is spot on when applied to the wage gap. BAME women are also more likely to be asked about our plans relating to marriage and pregnancy by prospective employers than white women. White women are objectified by men, the result of misogyny. Women of colour are objectified, Othered, fetishised, and treated like hypersexual savages by men, the result of misogyny and racism. BAME and migrant women also "experience a disproportionate rate of domestic homicide."

Even if you are not prepared to listen to what women of colour have to say about racism, the facts and figures bear out.

'Women are stronger when we all stand together.'

Yes. Sisterhood is a powerful, sustaining force. But expecting women of colour to remain silent on the subject of race for the sake of white comfort is not sisterhood—quite the opposite. Sisterhood cannot exist so long as white women continue to ignore the hierarchy of race whilst simultaneously expecting women of colour to devote our energies solely to helping them gain equality with white men. This paradigm is exploitative, a toxic manifestation of white entitlement within the feminist movement.

For sisterhood to exist between women of colour and white women, we must have an honest conversation about race within the feminist movement. White privilege must be acknowledged and opposed by white women. Whiteness must cease to be treated as the normative standard of womanhood within feminist politics. The same logic that is applied to critiquing misogyny must be applied to unlearning racism. Issues facing women of colour must be considered a priority, not a distraction to be dealt with after the revolution. Women of colour must cease to be treated like a box-ticking exercise and instead acknowledged for what we are, what we have always been: essential to the feminist movement.

All this is imperative if we are to achieve true solidarity—and that is possible. As things stand, the onus is on white women to reach out and repair any rift that occurs on the basis of race. Ultimately, it will bring us all closer to liberation.

BIBLIOGRAPHY

Davis, A., 1981. *Women, Race & Class.* New York: Vintage.

Grewal, S. ed., 1988. *Charting the Journey: Writings by Black and Third World Women.* London: Sheba Feminist Press.

Hill Collins, P., 2000. *Black Feminist Thought.* New York: Routledge.

hooks, b., 1984. *Feminist Theory: From Margin to Center.* Cambridge, MA: South End Press.

hooks, b., 2000. *Feminism is for Everybody: Passionate Politics.* New York: Routledge.

Lorde, A., 1984. *Sister Outsider: Essays and Speeches.* Berkeley: Crossing Press.

Wallace, M., 1978. *Black Macho and the Myth of Superwoman.* New York: The Dial Press.

An Indian woman by Sunayna Pal

I have a hunched back

Not that I am very tall

my mom was worried I was growing too much

and no boy would come for me

I have hair on my lips which isn't approved by society

I am tired of removing it

in moments of anger,

I feel like removing my upper lip instead.

I have tried to prevent hairfall.

with eggs curds and powders

I want smooth shiny hair like they show in movies

but all this has resulted in hair fall

I have my odours and smells

on my special days and otherwise

I don't know why I protect it with perfume

Ironically, I don't like it myself

An Indian woman

I have supportive husband and uncles

but critical aunts and angry sisters

I hear my neighbour upset with her husband

and a part of me feels good

This is the part that needs healing

This is why there is rape

It is because of me.

It is when I compete with other women

Women empowerment is a far-fetched dream

until I do something with myself

I need to love myself

I need to accept myself

The Outsider Within: Racism in the Feminist Movement by Claire Heuchan

A brief foreword: this essay is the second in a series on race and racism in the feminist movement. It is a work of personal reflection. No individuals, organisations, or events are/will be named or directly identified. My objective is neither to call out nor to heap praise on any woman, but rather to highlight some realities of interracial dynamics between women in feminism.

The personal is political. So goes the rallying cry of second wave feminism, a perspective which has characterised a significant body of feminist theory. It is for this reason that I have decided to share a reflection upon my experience as a Black woman within the movement. There is a theory within Black feminism that being an outsider on the grounds of both race and sex positions Black women as watchers, gives us particular insight into dominant power structures and the means by which they manifest (Hill Collins, 2000). With this in mind, I aim to live up to the standards set by my foremothers and improve this movement for the women of colour who will follow after me.

Feminism is for everybody—so says bell hooks. (Note: hooks is not arguing that the movement should prioritise men, or any other dominant class, but rather be fully inclusive on grounds of race, class, and sexuality.) This text was critical in my development of a Black radical feminism, the moment when black became Black. *Feminism is for Everybody* outlined the importance of acknowledging race and class alongside sex if white supremacist capitalist patriarchy is to be dismantled, and provided a blueprint for true interracial solidarity between women. Here, hooks posited that sisterhood can exist between women of colour and white women provided that race is acknowledged as a hierarchy, racism as a system of power, from which white women benefit. If white women continue to deny the privilege of whiteness, disregarding countless testimonies delivered by women of colour, we have no reason to trust them as political allies—this is hooks' perspective, and one with which I agree wholeheartedly.

Interracial solidarity between women is possible. I know. I have experienced it. But I have also learned that it is so rare, the alternative so uncomfortable, that I will never condemn another woman of colour for claiming otherwise. This solidarity is by no means guaranteed—in my opinion, it is safer never to expect it—but it is powerful when it goes right.

The Outsider Within: Racism in the Feminist Movement

The first place I experienced true interracial solidarity within the movement is the women's organisation where I volunteer. The values and praxis of this organisation are intersectional in the purest sense—it is a place for women of colour, working class women, lesbian and bi women, women with disabilities. Women negotiating marginalised identities are not treated like tokens, or a box to be ticked off for funding purposes: we are at the heart of the organisation. The longer I am there, the more I appreciate this. The longer I am there, the more uncommon I realise this situation actually is. It is a place where I can sit around a table working with white women and know that they do not view my Blackness as an easy method of virtue-signalling, something to be displayed when convenient and disregarded when it is not. Difference isn't fetishised or ignored, but acknowledged and treated accordingly—exactly the criteria outlined by hooks. These are women who live their feminist principles, and I am proud to work alongside them.

It is worth observing that the majority of white women with whom I share solidarity are significantly older than me, and/or lesbian, and/or working class. As to why these women tend to be older, feminism was significantly more radical when they started down the path of activism, which undoubtedly shaped their perspective on structural oppression. Radically feminist politics added depth to their structural analysis, to the extent that bypassing race became both extremely difficult to justify and intellectually dishonest.

It is easy to answer the lesbian part of this dynamic—in her novel *The Night Watch*, Sarah Waters postulated that lesbians tend to show one another "gallantry" on the grounds that nobody else will and, broadly speaking, I think that she is right. In some cases these are women who fought Section 28—it's reasonable to imagine they now watch the babydykes flourish and consider it an achievement. Having experienced considerable marginalisation themselves, these women are more likely to be conscious of the marginalisation experienced by others—how intersectionality is supposed to, but does not always, work.

Why I find easier kinship with white working class women is also clear. They are consciously unlearning racism as I (a Black middle class woman) am consciously unlearning classism. As multiple works of feminist scholarship have argued, race and class are inextricably linked by dominant structures of power. Neither Black nor working class features in the rosy picture of life in the UK as painted by the Little Britain mentality. We both belong to the parts of society rendered other, over there, not quite People Like the hegemonic 'Us'. White working class women have engaged with my activism and shown me extraordinary kindness in a way that, to my thinking, exemplifies sisterhood.

These women have shown me every personal and professional consideration. They have encouraged my work, amplified my voice, and listened closely to what I have to say. They are my sisters. They have my trust. And they are the exception to the rule of white racism.

Participating in the feminist movement as a Black woman is, frankly, difficult. That's not because of the MRAs and right-wing racists who are routinely overwhelmed by the urge to call me nigger, suggest that I "go back to Africa" (FYI: impossible—to my regret, I've never actually visited that continent, and they are never willing to follow through by funding my plane tickets…), make some allusion to slavery or the Ku Klux Klan in the hope of causing me discomfort, etc. These people are irrelevant. Over time, I have grown desensitised to such attacks. No, what makes my participation in feminism difficult is witnessing and experiencing the racism of white women I had previously considered allies—women who understand misogyny on a structural level, yet turn a blind eye to racism. They have been responsible for every one of the numerous points at which I have wanted to leave the movement, to distance myself from what I know to be a vital cause.

Whenever I discuss race, the result is the same. White, self-proclaimed feminist women have sworn at me, spoken over me, questioned my feminist credentials, mocked me, made thinly-veiled racist jokes, and—most bizarrely—policed my race. So quickly, white defensiveness evolves into white cruelty. I will not give examples. I will not include screencaps, or name and shame the culprits. What I will say is that it happens regularly enough that I am automatically on guard with white feminist women, just waiting for the microaggressions to begin. And they do.

Some white feminists even feel compelled to set little tests, which I can pass only by demonising Black men and prioritising sex over race in my analysis. I can't even indulge in that petty internet pastime of commenting on Kanye West's antics without some white woman showing up in my mentions, expecting me to a) monster Black masculinity b) stop listening to his music c) distance myself from Black culture in the name of sisterhood. If I critique the misogynoir directed towards Black women in the music industry, such as Nicki Minaj, the response is similarly predictable. White women gloss over the way Nicki repeatedly encourages her female fans to focus on their education and never depend upon a man, they ignore the message behind her music and the way it uplifts Black womanhood—they only want to critique the sexuality of her image. Bonus points if Taylor Swift is held up in contrast as a good role model for girls.

And then there are the white women who view associating with me as a fast-track to cookies. "I can't be racist: I have a Black friend!" On multiple occasions, white feminists have tagged me in

The Outsider Within: Racism in the Feminist Movement

their Twitter arguments with racists, often exposing me to graphic images and racist language in the process. They do this with less thought towards me than Ash Ketchum ever showed a Pokémon he sent into battle. They do it in the belief that I will fight on their behalf, use my voice to provide them with the moral high ground. I will not. Images of white violence against Black people are deeply unsettling. That entitlement towards my intellectual labour is an act of contempt. It is dehumanising, accompanied by a real disregard for my wellbeing.

It is impossible to feel solidarity with women who expect me to downplay and ignore my Blackness and its political implications for their comfort. I cannot feel sisterhood with women who expect me to stay silent because it's "just race", dismissing a system of oppression that continues to shape my life as "a distraction". There is no room for trust on my side when I am constantly deflecting racism. When I talk about race and feminism with other women of colour, they know. They instinctively get it. There is no need to explain, and that is a wonderful thing in a world where garden variety bigots and white feminists alike are directing racism our way.

Yet, I cannot bring myself to give up on the vision of a united feminist movement. The white women with whom I share solidarity have all worked to achieve that level of consciousness. They show that racism does not have to be a barrier between women if we are all committed to challenging white supremacy. In Angela Davis' autobiography, there is a particularly touching passage in which she reveals her mother's commitment to interracial solidarity in the struggle against all forms of oppression. Sallye Davis' generosity of spirit, the strength she showed in having kept such hope alive, are inspirational.

If I am willing to remain an optimist, it is because I believe in a feminist movement built upon true solidarity—one in which "all women" means "all women", not an insistence that white women are prioritised. It's not here today, but it can be. When white women are ready to put in the work, I will be prepared to call them sister.

BIBLIOGRAPHY

Davis, A. 1974. *An Autobiography*. New York: Random House.

hooks, b., 1984. *Feminist Theory: From Margin to Center*. Cambridge, MA: South End Press.

hooks, b., 2000. *Feminism is for Everybody: Passionate Politics*. New York: Routledge.

Hill Collins, P., 2000. *Black Feminist Thought*. New York: Routledge.

Smith, B., 1998. *The Truth That Never Hurts: Writings on Race, Gender and Freedom*. New Brunswick: Rutgers University Press.

Waters, S., 2006. *The Night Watch*. London: Virago.

Abortion by Erika Garrett

I started a petition in November 2014 calling for buffer zones to be created outside abortion clinics. BPAS (British Pregnancy Advisory Service) also named me as one of their champions of choice for my campaigning after presenting the petition to No.10. Sadly, I haven't been able to bring about change ... Yet!

I am heartened by the continued news coverage of abortion clinics and by research stating how most women do not regret their abortions (please read the article by Rebecca Schiller on the statistics at the end of this post).

I'm going to be clear and say that I will not use the term 'anti-choice' (even though protestors are anti choice) as abortion is not a dirty word. I spoke to a researcher from BBC R4 (sadly they didn't run with the piece) about the stigma and taboo surrounding abortion. Women feel shamed into keeping their abortions secret, this should not be the case. Many of us would be open about having a medical procedure without fear of recrimination. Having an abortion is a medical procedure too, it really is that simple. So women should have safe access to medical help.

Despite what anti abortion protestors would like you to think...

Abortion is legal up to 24 weeks.

Late abortions are very rare.

Abortion is not murder.

No baby or child has been killed.

Women are not ignorant of their decisions. Many women already have children and even if they haven't, women can be trusted to make their own choices over their bodies.

Abortion saves lives! I can't imagine the pain a woman would go through having to give birth to an unwanted baby. Not to mention the life that baby may go on to have.

I may well be preaching to the converted here but I feel I need to keep posting blogs on this issue as it is not going away. Buffer zones are the only practical answer to the blight and upset that anti abortion protestors cause. They may have a right to protest but they do not have the right to cause upset and harass women and staff just because they don't like it!

Room For Our Anger

Cyborg by Susan Dunsford

I am a cyborg in the cyborg world. Since my creation I have been programmed and controlled. My rulers pretend that I have free will, but they are adept at ensuring that the things I want are the things that they want me to want. I make choices and proclaim my Self an individual, but there are many like me, making the same choices, declaring the same free choice. The people who want me to 'choose' their products are fascinated by how I make those choices. They will study my type, and then process the perfect product for me. When I am at the store, I will then 'choose' their product. I feel like I am making a choice, but really I am following an advanced program.

My rulers pretend that I have free will and much is made of the ability to think and choose for oneself. But there are harsh penalties for those who do not make the right choices. A man who wants to work in childcare? Pervert and paedophile. A woman who wants to excel in the work place? A man in the wrong costume. And those are the mild epithets and punishments. Imagine how harsh the penalty for those who do not conduct their 'private' lives according to the rules. For our private lives are most public of all.

Those cyborgs who follow the rules and become successful become the next generation of rulers. Climb to the top and they will hold the front page, let you take center stage. The media, so beguiling that it is hard to draw the line between our real lives and the virtual entities we consume, is the chief mouthpiece for the rules. We do not need overblown images of our rulers on the street corners, mouths opening, proclaiming their wisdom, telling us that they are watching us, but they are there. Celebrities, nonentities, those who conform with ease, they stare down at us, telling us what to buy, say, do, be, in order to be just like them. The media spews forth its rules, and we believe them. We see an endless array of images, showing us perfection, telling us to dress like that and walk this way. We pay good money to hear the wit and wisdom of these rulers. And all the time, the cyborgs who have conformed to their programming, are stretched before us, their mouths agape in an endless-seeming 'O' of oppression. O for obsequious, obedience and Oh do stop moaning and go for a spa day, dear.

Oh My! So, I have followed my programming and I fit the pattern. I have a typical career, a child, a tastefully decorated house and a husband. By following the program, I have become reliant, financially dependent, enslaved by the hour, and I am approved of. To break the program, to break free, is almost unthinkable. There are two cars in the garage and a chicken in the pot, so I have got my lot.

My very existence is a part of the program, and perpetuates it. I am publicly seen to conform, and that provides a role model to younger cyborgs. No matter what words I use, my dress, my job, my life, show that I have conformed. I have received enough success that I spread the message: follow the rules and you too could have a comfortable life. I have traded much in the way of integrity to achieve security. For such is our society; non-conformists sacrifice their security. So, I stand in front of the class and hammer the lesson home. Be on time. Bam. Turn in your work. Bam. Dress appropriately. Bam. Think for yourself. Bam. But only the thoughts that we want you to think. Double bam. Class is done, and 'thank you ma'am'.

With all this careful programming, there is little chance to break the code.

Songs proclaim that "I can watch a sunset on my own"; Sarah Bareilles tells us that Cinderella is on the floor, that she doesn't care about our fairy tales. There are signs that we do not blindly follow our programming, that people will challenge our assumptions. These are small steps. The happy ever after of Disney and the rom-com still outsell these cult-status pieces of culture. There has always been a niche market for the different of thinking, this is nothing new. It provides a useful safety-valve. We have the illusion of freedom of choice and freedom of thinking, but really the power stays with the rulers, and they can neatly identify those who do not conform; label and distance them, then blame them for the choices that they make.

At work I stand at the front of the room, a role model of the happy family wife. Learn your lessons well, children, and you could be just like me. Bam.

You women! You're such bitches by Cath Bore

We're frequently told, aren't we, that women don't like other women, we hasten to criticize, we're eager to pounce on any alleged flaw, blood in the water attracting the sharks. The female to female viewpoint is followed by a rolling of the eyes like an echo, with an exclamation of "You women! You're such bitches!" The term "bitch" is misogynistic and thrown about with abandon. Any comment by a woman is bitching. A conversation between two women, that's bitching. Two bitches bitching. A woman expressing an opinion that means she's a bitch, yeah? Another bitch bitching again. Bitch is part of our discourse. Bitch is a woman, bitch is talk, bitching is women talking. We've totally fallen for it. Men talking, a man commenting on another man is unremarkable, of course. No eye rolling there, no bitching. Silence everyone, nod your head and furrow your bitching brow. Keep on walking, there's nothing to see here. Don't question, bitches. We've fallen for that too, we've fallen for the denial of sisterhood. It's crept up on us, bitches.

I am the compere at an open mic night. I introduce singers, poets, storytellers who come along to entertain and be heard each month. Open mics provide an open forum and a microphone in pubs and cafés, for anyone wanting to perform. Sounds nice, doesn't it? Those who don't go to open mics might imagine them romantic affairs, strumming minstrels and acoustic loveliness, Bob Dylan thoughtfulness and earnest songwriters. In the real world, though, open mic events are notoriously curious and sometimes hostile affairs, competitive and sneery, my guitar's bigger and better than yours, male-dominated. Me though, I run a comfortably tight ship. Just call me Captain Bitch. No one talks when the acts are on, or dares leave after they've performed. Applause is mandatory. We have a full house right until the end.

Last month, one of the women putting her name forward to sing was a service user at our local hospital's mental health unit. She wanted to sing the song Valerie by Liverpool indie band The Zutons, not only solo but acapella too. A brave decision, even if I could sing I wouldn't do it on my own with no accompaniment. The whole premise to me feels vulnerable, naked. I don't have the backbone. The woman's performance started well but she forgot the words of the second verse. That could've been the end of it, but no. Instead of sniggering and being "bitchy" as eye rollers would love, three young women from a youth group got up, walked across the floor and stood with this visibly upset and distressed woman, and sang the song with her. Sisters, truly.

It was beautiful, and not just the singing. A simple gesture and unremarkable on the surface, but powerful true sisterhood in action, nudging its way in like the lemon light of early morning warms, nourishes. There's nothing to eye roll at, here. No bitching, bitches. It's sisterhood, sisters, and it goes on all the time, we just need to choose to see it.

The Colour of Justice by Estella Muzito

The sting of the blade crawled across my forehead. I felt the flesh curl away as the tingling spread the closer it got to bone and my head was swathed in fire.

"It's just as well," she said. "No man wants to look at you anyway, woman of the gutter."

I turned away from the stale stench oozing out of her toothless face. Tobacco laced with turmeric.

"Look at me when I'm talking to you!" she barked.

It was then that she began raining blows over my breasts; cursing me for being a waste of space in her home. By the time she had used up all the energy in her saggy arms, my whole body had been set alight. Through the stickiness of tears and blood that had glued shut parts of my eyelids, I could see figures hovering. They mumbled words that were not directed at me but were about me. Their eyes shifty like those of good people when they encountered a leper on the street. The night played out its time as I lay curled up on the cold cement floor.

I thought about Hamid and quickly struggled to stop myself. It was wrong to think about the dead with anything but good thoughts. I lifted a numb arm to my abdomen. Perhaps the witch was right, I thought. What kind of woman could go through life with as much misfortune unless if she was herself the devil?

"She is a good person," Hamid had pleaded once more for my understanding the last time I had sulked in our room following another clash. "You will get to love each other, soon."

"When will that be?" I had demanded between sobs, "I've lived in this home for a little over three years and things only get worse."

"A little more patience, darling," he had said as he walked over and held me. "She is probably still bitter about Neela's shameful departure."

"Hamid, your brother is already remarried; your mother and everyone else swiftly moved on. In any case, I should have gone away with Neela."

"You don't mean that," he had whispered as he turned up my chin and our eyes locked. "*Insh'Allah*, once the new operation is approved we will move up north and into our own home."

That's all that had kept me going those months before the fateful accident that had brought into my life more darkness than any one human being could endure in a lifetime. Hamid had been his father's favorite son. I too had become Baba's favorite—Neela had come before me. But she didn't make it. She couldn't have made it; she was too big-headed. I envied her for that and hated her at the same time. After all, it was to me that she had left the burden of the man of the house that was now full of ghosts.

It hadn't always been this way. There had been some laughter in the home, especially when we hosted the extended family during the annual week-long religious festivities. And always, in this very place, there had been the promise of life; at one time in my body as well. But that had ended not too long before the train accident that had taken Hamid away from me. A kind and gentle soul, he had left a vacuum so wide. Sun rays ceased to brighten the home, so much that even Hamid's self-involved roguish brother could not hide the anguish he felt at the loss.

Hamid and Kamal were as different as snow is from desert sand. Where Hamid was soft-spoken and driven, his elder brother was one of those men for whom being humble was to lack power. He had failed to reconcile how his laziness was to blame for the fact that Baba had chosen to place Hamid high in the ranks of the family business. For a while, it had caused an enormous rift in the family since traditionally, the elder son was expected to take over his father's matters. Ever the shrewd businessman, Baba had early on identified Hamid as the one most likely to keep his great grandfather's textile company operational for the next generation. None of Mama's pleas on Kamal's behalf had yielded much. The estrangement over what Kamal saw as his birthright went on to cause tension between my sister-in-law, Neela, and me. It was unfortunate for us. For me being the newest in the home, and for her as she struggled to exist in a world dominated by the physical and egotistic needs of Kamal and his father. We had drawn closer in the year that she decided to take her destiny into her own hands. By then Hamid had grasped the workings of textile trading and in no time embarked on the expansion plan that promised a move for us away from the family home. And then fate struck. In truth, it had come long before Hamid's death.

* * *

"We will break off for a half hour recess," the speaker of the council announced after nearly half of us had taken to the podium.

The Security Council convened every three months to listen to the citizens' grievances. It was a nine-member, all-female body representing people from different walks of life; women, men, and

The Colour of Justice

children. The new government had set it up to deal with the decades-thick backlog in the courts of law. That day, about fifty women and a handful of men from within the neighboring communities took up the reserved seats up front, awaiting their turn to be heard. The scars were evident: for many of the women on their foreheads, like mine. More symbols were speckled over the parts of their bodies that were not covered up in *kangas*.

As each one recounted their case to the bench, the rest looked on in silence. It seemed like we were out of tears. All we needed was an ear from Lady Justice. Some of the women in attendance had been abandoned on the streets, and others thrown out of matrimonial homes for the crime of bearing only girls. Old women, gray, and bent, battered by their own sons; the price for having dead husbands. Women of all ages cast out of their clans, bruised and battered, for one senseless fault or the other. Finally, it was my turn to speak. The story was old. The scars were raw. But we had all cried enough. We were no longer weak.

It was a clear day with a beautiful sky, the monsoon having ended not too long ago. On the boundaries of the courtyard where the hearing was taking place, under the shade of a neat row of jacaranda in purple glory, vendors had set up stalls selling flavored water and salty snacks. I stretched, having sat for too long. I had no money, but it didn't matter now that I had made it here.

Two of the men who had spoken so far stood deep in conversation a row ahead of me, to my left. "We can only rely on their empathy, and hope for the best," one of them said with a sorrowful look on a once well-fed face that was now framed by dirty white sideburns.

"Everything I did was at the behest of people like them," he carried on as his eyes swept over the crowd. "There's no reason why my family and practice were destroyed for providing a public service."

The other looked at him and raised his arms in despair. "One can only hope that in another world there'll be a council that's more attuned to our concerns. In this regime we have no choice but to take what's given."

"Then what is the point if it doesn't speak to fairness!" his companion shrieked.

As they carried on the expressive chatter, a lady who had spoken after me walked over smiling as though we were old friends at a wedding party. I remembered seeing her right before the hearing; her gait stiff, and the evidence of insomnia shadowing her face. She now had the look of someone from whom a heavy load had been lifted. Her eyes sparkled as she drew closer.

"Sister, I heard of the horrors you suffered," she said, squeezing my right arm.

"And I, yours. May it be that we find healing." I acknowledged our shared predicament with a smile.

"You won't find healing here," she retorted, catching me unaware with the change of tone.

"Sorry?" I asked. Certain that I'd heard her wrong.

"You heard me right, there's no justice here. We have to find it for ourselves."

"Then why did you bring your grievances to the council?" I asked.

By this time, the patrons around the stalls had significantly fizzled out. Slowly, people were trickling back to their seats. My mouth was dry, and I could feel my heartbeat rise. Perhaps sensing the discomfort I was in, she promptly offered to buy me a pouch of vanilla water.

"I've come for him," she said as she pointed with her twisted mouth to the two men I had overheard earlier.

"What do you mean, you've come for him? Who is he to you?" Suddenly I was filled with dread at the thought of dealing with a mad woman.

"He is dead to me, but in another life, he was my family's GP."

"What do you want from him, except to grant forgiveness for whatever may have happened in the past and move on?"

"I will do that when the scar on my forehead vanishes. Until then, I'm here for vengeance," she barked and walked off.

The rest of the hearing flew by without me dwelling too much on the other witness accounts. I couldn't erase the nameless woman from my head. I sensed her wrath, and I wanted to bask in it. It was inevitable that I sought her out and we made a plan.

Just as we laid down the path to vengeance, I woke up to find myself still on the cement floor; my body burning from the blows and cuts of another bleeding night filled with the muted snores of the people I called my loved ones.

* * *

Now Baba too was gone. The doctor had said that it was due to an unhealthy lifestyle. If only the man of medicine knew. Kamal and his family had long moved to the southern districts to pursue his latest venture in the mining towns. Only Mama and I were left to live within the dilapidated walls. I had taken to selling sweet ices by the roadside. It was especially lucrative in the humid months as old and young alike sought some relief from the harshness of the sun. Back at the house, the passage of time had exercised its tendency to make life a bit bearable. But not even brittle bones could cure Mama of the hatred she had for me. Neither did the passing years take from me the dream and the words of that mad woman whose lips had dripped with retribution. I no longer wondered what the doctor had done to her. My eyes and ears had grown weary. I had graduated from the green nineteen-year-old that had walked through these doors with a smile and the dream of happily-ever-after.

I craved for the day we would all be given some justice. I knew that it could only come in that utopia I had dreamt about. So mostly, I mused over the plans we had made for vengeance. This was the color of justice in the world I lived in. Sometimes as I massaged Mama's swollen legs in the evenings, I thought of squeezing harder so that the blood circulation was cut from her feet upwards. And every other day as I made her morning meal, I imagined how I could take that dream to its final conclusion. These thoughts filled up my mind and fueled my body, as Hamid and Baba, Neela and Kamal, all drifted in the past.

* * *

Mama cleared her throat as she appeared in the doorway. She moved slowly to the settee, sat down and tapped her lap; a signal to mean that she wanted to fix my hair. I sat by her feet and she tenderly oiled and plaited my locks. Mama hated me for reasons we both could never reconcile. But we only had each other in a world that had stolen all that we could have been. We kept one another going—for good and evil. There was enough justice in the house of ghosts after   all.

Room For Ourselves

Sister, mother by Lorrie Hartshorn

Sister, mother, I feel your pain

Scalding rage on stinging face, heart on fire

Hollow thunder beneath your ribs

Where once your round, peaceful egg.

You swelled with your fruit

cradling warmth and new life

constructed in the heart of you

eating the heart of you

right from your hand.

Sister, mother,

You are a warrior, a queen, whose precious tears

will nourish the child and the ground

in which she grows.

Trust me now,

Sister, mother,

When I tell you: you are beautiful in your rage

Your pain is your glory, your capacity, your depth

From which new life has sprung

You astound.

You have given her life, set her free in the world

Sister, mother

Your arms hold her now as your womb held before

And while you are shaken to the roots of your self

Know they run deep and will hold you

like a mother.

And while storms break inside you and shatter your bones

and scatter the pieces of you on her cheek with your tears,

know you are glorious

descended from one, the rock to another

giver of life,

Sister, mother.

Because Ogwugwu Said So by Egoyibo Okoro

The shrine of Ogwugwu was hidden in a part of Umueze village that nobody dared to visit, except those who came to seek truth and an end to their problems.

The forest used to be a burial ground for those that had defiled the land: twins whose only crime was being born as two from their mother's womb, incestuous daughters who had seduced their fathers, traitors who had betrayed their people, slaves who had refused to be obedient, and those who committed *ochu*. They were often buried alive.

Many heard the wailing of spirits, the unsettled souls who cried for redemption, to be granted funerals in keeping with the laws of the land. Ghosts were seen wandering around these parts, dumb and sad-looking.

Ifunanya had never seen a ghost, not even when her mother died two years ago did she see or hear from her spirit, although everybody else reported seeing her.

Her mother had died a horrifying death, killed by one of those new machines people from the city rode in—the ones they called motorcars—as she was crossing the road.

Even though she was given a funeral befitting her status as *Lolo*—the wife of a titled man—her spirit had wandered the earth refusing to go to the land of the dead, until the high priest of Ogwugwu had come to enchant her grave and drive her to the spirit world.

Ifunanya prayed not to see any ghosts as it would be too frightening and the memory would stay with her forever. Being dragged by her husband and two men of his family to see Ogwugwu was terrifying enough.

Who knows what Ogwugwu will say? Why am I afraid? Surely the gods do not lie.

She certainly didn't want the emotional burden of encountering a ghost. Scared, she gripped her husband Ngwu's hand. To her surprise, he squeezed it back and smiled at her.

He had been cold with her, ever since his mother blamed their three years of childlessness on the fact that she might be an *ogbanje*. After all, she was as beautiful and fair as the women who were said to come from the spirit world to torment their loved ones.

How ridiculous!

However, Ngwu had taken the suggestion to heart and made arrangements for them to see the mighty oracle, Ogwugwu. Now she was scared he would send her away if the oracle would say that she could not bear children.

"Ifunanya, why are you clinging to Ngwu like a pumpkin leaf to the stem? Are you scared?" her father-in-law, Pa Okoye, teased.

Everybody laughed.

"No, papa, I'm holding him so I don't fall," she lied.

"Tah! I know you lie. But I forgive you. This forest sings silent sorrowful songs saturated in tragedies. Were it not for my strength as a man, I would have clung to my brother, Mazi Omenka here."

They all laughed. Pa Okoye was a funny man, a good man. He was tall and well-built like his son Ngwu, but lacked the serious manner that made Ngwu a ruthless hunter, fierce wrestler, breaker of maidens' hearts and a formidable enemy. Pa Okoye had made his riches as a craftsman, weaving mats, hand-fans and wall arts that were shipped to faraway lands and sold to white men.

They reached the enclave that marked the entrance to Ogwugwu's shrine. The gong or *ogene* could be heard accompanied by high-pitched melodious chants of *Onye Ozi*, the high priest of Ogwugwu, a small odious man whom many feared for his prophetic position as the seer of the revered god.

They stood before the shrine, waiting admittance.

Onye Ozi was dancing, or rather whirling in circles, chanting in a somewhat foreign language. It sounded like the Ibo language but no word could be deciphered from his mutterings. The altar was decorated with peacock feathers, a tall carved stool, small moulded pots, a snarling cat that had been dried and preserved, and a large calabash filled with clear water.

Ifunanya wondered how he did it—this non-stop whirling—without falling or showing signs of dizziness.

Abruptly, he stopped. With his back to them and facing *Alusi* Ogwugwu, he shouted, "Ogwugwu, they've come. Be kind and speak before the child dies of hunger in his mother's

Because Ogwugwu Said So

presence. For, a fly without a counsellor heads to the grave with the corpse. Speak, great one, speak!"

He turned around and gestured for them to come in and sit before him. They removed their sandals and sat on the wide multi-coloured hand-woven mat in Ogwugwu's shrine.

Ifunanya sat beside Ngwu with her hand still in his.

Pa Okoye cleared his throat, greeted Ogwugwu, their ancestors and Onye Ozi, before saying: "The seer of Ogwugwu, we have come to seek your help. Our people say, 'that which an adult sees sitting, the child will not see even when he stands up and cranes his neck'."

Pausing for effect, he continued, "My son Ngwu has been married for three years now without child. Not for lack of trying for he is a virile man. His wife he met a virgin, yet the cries of the wee ones have not been heard in their household…"

Onye Ozi cut in harshly. "I know why you've come, the great one revealed all. Ogwuwu said to warn you to not give this young woman–" his gaze swept Ifunanya, "–a hard time. She loves her husband, and he loves her. She is not the cause of her childlessness."

Ifunanya looked up to the heavens and thanked *Olisa bi n'igwe.*

He hummed, bent and rattled some cowries spread out before him before continuing. "A long time ago, there was a girl that was kidnapped, raped by her cousins and later sold to an *onye ocha*—a white man, who then sold her to another *onye ocha*, a farmer in a faraway land where she was maltreated until she died in childbirth. Her spirit wanders the earth, refusing to rest until she has avenged her death. She has sworn that none will bear fruit except if she wishes it."

Mouth agape, Ngwu made to speak but his uncle Mazi Omenka forestalled him.

"I know of my father's sister who was said to have gone missing when she was seventeen. She had gone to the farm one day but never came back. They searched extensively but nobody seemed to know her whereabouts. It was as if she had disappeared from the face of the earth."

Pa Okoye recalled, "Surely, wise one, something can be done to appease her?"

His right eye closed, Onye Ozi looked into a small calabash of water before him with his left *nzu* painted eye. Shaking his head, he stood up to kneel before the two feet and finely sculpted fierce-looking face that was an image of Ogwugwu. He muttered incoherent words and bobbed his head. Then he sat back on the mat and chuckled. "She's a feisty one. She asks for much. Too much. But Ogwugwu has spoken and she must obey!"

He chanted for a full minute, using the dozen or so cowries before him to draw zigzagged and circular lines on the mat. "To appease her, you must bring a cow, two four-year-old he-goats, sixteen tubers of the new yam, a head of palm-nut, a bunch of unripe plantain, a head of kola-nuts, and twenty bags of cowries, before the next *Eke* market day." He paused to stare at Ifunanya who gasped at the long list of expensive items.

She edged closer to Ngwu and he hugged her.

"And you must dig a grave and bury her. She mourns the absence of a proper funeral—as is her right as *nwaokpu*—a daughter of the tribe. If you do all these, it will be well with your family again. You may leave. Ogwugwu has spoken."

He rapped his knuckles on the *ogene* beside him, bent his head and closed his eyes like one in a trance.

Pa Okoye bowed. "Thank you, wise one. Thank you."

They left, sombre and deep in thought.

Ifunanya was silent but inwardly she was happy, too happy, to be worried about the long list of expensive items required to appease the *nwaokpu*. Her father-in-law was equal to the task. He had more money than the village chief.

Thank the gods it wasn't her fault they were childless after all.

GLOSSARY

Alusi Oracle.

Eke One of the four market days that made up a week in the Igbo calendar.

Igwe Village chief.

Lolo The wife of a titled man.

Nwaokpu Daughter.

Nzu A local white chalk.

Ochu Murder.

Ogbanje An evil child who shuttles between the land of the living and the spirit world.

Ogene A small gong.

Olisa bi n'igwe The progenitor of Igbo race who lives in heaven.

Onye ocha A white man.

Onye Ozi Informant/Seer/Servant.

Giving birth in a dictatorship by Erika Garrett

I was inspired to write this after reading a tweet about couples having sex shortly before or after giving birth. Sex was the last thing on my mind when I gave birth!!

I'm writing this for all the women out there who did not have the nice rose-tinted birth that we all wish for. To put things into context, I have three children and two different dads. My son was born when I was 20 and I had been on my own since I was 8 weeks pregnant.

I won't bore you with the gruesome details of that birth but let's just say it wasn't pleasant and resulted in me needing a blood transfusion and my son needing UV (jaundice). Whilst my son's dad was a waste of space, he was never abusive. Having said that, I didn't want him at the birth as I had been through the pregnancy alone.

Before, during and after the birth he managed to gain access to me by saying that he was my partner! This caused me great distress and I asked the staff to not allow him in. The note on the phone got thrown away and so he walked back onto the ward using the 'I'm her partner' line (the staff member responsible for this gave me a very teary apology). I can't remember exactly what I said to him but I do know that I screamed at him to leave.

When I met my ex husband I was so excited to find out that I was pregnant, we'd been together only 7 months. I always wanted to have more than one child and it pained me to see all my friends having their second or third child. When it came to giving birth, it was so much better than my first. I can honestly say that I thought I had won the lottery…

Things went downhill when it came to kicking out time. My ex didn't want to go and I was already quite reliant on him so was terrified at the thought of coping alone. He had a massive argument with one of the midwives as he refused to go home. This resulted in me crying, I couldn't stand to see him being so horrible to these women. The midwife decided that he could stay but it left me feeling distraught and isolated.

When I found out I was pregnant with my third child, I immediately worried about the birth. The whole pregnancy was spent with my ex going on and on about me coming straight home and me fretting about his behaviour. The domestic abuse had really taken a hold by then although I was very much in denial.

Giving birth in a dictatorship

My third child was born and the midwife said I could go home after a couple of hours of recovery. My ex was over the moon, I was relieved even though I wanted to stay the night... Then I had a massive bleed... Nothing serious or life-threatening but enough for them to tell me they wanted to admit me and the baby. This sent my ex over the edge.

Once in a room on the ward, he seemed agitated and stressed. This made me feel very unsettled. I was in such a mess that it took me quite a while to phone my family about the birth. It was almost like the birth never happened, my priority was to keep my ex happy and calm. On a trip to the toilet I lost more blood and became tachycardic. I was put straight onto IV fluids and told to rest. Well...

My ex descended into a rage as now I needed to stay the night. He punched and head butted the walls and then he left me stranded. Little did I know that he went to the pub... I can't describe how upset I was, how much emotional pain I felt. The midwife came to do my obs and I begged her to be allowed home.

I told her how upset he was and I cried so much I thought I might never stop. The doctor came and said I should stay in so I had to discharge myself. Lo and behold, this made my ex very happy.

I wonder how many other women have silently suffered like I did? Who can't tell the truth about the birth because they want everyone to think it was wonderful and amazing. How they feel robbed of beautiful memories. How this most precious of moments becomes another story of him???

The birth of my third child should have been about me and the baby. We both got utterly forgotten; it still upsets me now. I feel such sorrow when I think of my parents and my children turning up at the hospital, all excited to see the new baby, only to find we had gone home (ex didn't think to let them know so I had to apologise to them). Sorrow isn't a strong enough word, heartbroken is.

So stupid articles about how women are giving their partners blow jobs as a thank you for being at the birth, irritate the hell out of me. Giving birth should be a sacred experience. Putting aside the man in the equation, for me it felt like I had connected to all my ancestors who had been through labour before me.

Giving birth in a dictatorship

It was almost primitive. Those are the feelings that I should carry with me, not those of my vain efforts to placate an abusive man. What I'm trying to say, in a not very succinct way (!), is that giving birth should be about the woman and her baby, the man is a footnote (awaits backlash for that comment). Stop trying to accommodate the man and his needs in the delivery room—refocus on the woman.

Feminist Mothering with Fibromyalgia by Louise Pennington

I have fibromyalgia. I rarely admit to having it in public. If people ask why I look exhausted or am limping or struggling to use words, I say I have migraines. People have sympathy for migraines. They know it means extreme pain and sensitivities. When you say, "I have fibromyalgia" the response wavers between "I have a sore knee too" or "I've heard of that. My third-cousin twice-removed, next-door neighbour's parakeet's beautician has it and they got to go on disability for life." Neither response makes it possible to explain what fibromyalgia does to your body.

Fibromyalgia has been called the "aggravating everything disorder." I cannot control my body temperature. It doesn't matter what the weather is like outside, my body runs on its own internal thermostat which is, inevitably, wrong. I'm the one in the school playground in a t-shirt in the middle of winter and a hoodie on the hottest day of the year. I am also light sensitive, which means I'm also the one in sunglasses in the rain. My biggest 'aggravator' trigger is noise. When it is bad, the noise is so overwhelming that I can't differentiate sound. Everything is extreme. I wear headphones to drown the noise out.

My immune system goes on strike regularly and a mild runny nose can result in my being in bed for a week. The last time I had the flu, it took nearly 6 months to recover properly. I get every bug going and, sometimes, it feels like I am always sick. We won't discuss the side effects of the irritable bowel syndrome that co-exists with fibromyalgia.

A Facebook meme a few months ago made it clear: "my pain is not like your pain". I have pain every day—sometimes it's manageable with painkillers and heat pads and sometimes it's not. Sometimes I can't turn my head because the muscles have seized. On more than one occasion the pain at the base of my skull has been so severe that piercing the back of my neck with a knitting needle didn't seem like too bad an idea.

I've been really open about how hard it is as someone who loves writing to be unable to put my thoughts out coherently: that what ends up on the paper isn't what was in my head because of the way the fibromyalgia has effected the ability of my brain to communicate clearly. It's also affected my ability to speak since I lose words and have huge pauses in between words (that I don't realise are happening). I also find it difficult to process what is being said to me when tired: I know people are talking but I can't hear the actual words and, even when I can hear some of the words, my brain can't actually process the message. When it's this bad, the only thing I can do is nap. This isn't exactly conducive to being a writer.

It is the fatigue that is the worst symptom. Sleep deprivation is classed as a form of torture for a reason. I am often in a severe state of exhaustion. I can't sleep so the pain increases and because of the severity of the pain, I can't sleep. So, I have depression as well. The depression and severe pain require long-term medications, which result in weight gain. Weight gain makes it harder to exercise and the circle continues.

Obviously this pain and exhaustion impact on my daily life, but it is my mothering where it impacts the most. Living with fibromyalgia makes mothering nearly impossible. I can cope on school days when the pain is in a 'good' phase because I can nap during the day. Weekends are more difficult. I cannot manage the day without a nap which means I have to plan my time with my daughters around my sleep schedule. It is even worse when the pain is severe or I have a cold.

I have two daughters. My eldest was nine before I was diagnosed with fibromyalgia. I used to take her to castles, the zoo, and to the beach all the time. We would walk for miles in the woods, scramble up hills, and go camping. With my younger daughter, walking three blocks to school can result in a four-hour nap. Camping outside is a no-go since tense muscles and pain don't respond well to sleeping on the ground—and this is without dealing with the issue of my inability to control my body temperature.

How do you explain to a young child that the reason you can't listen to their story is because the distortion in your ears is so intense that you can't actually hear their words? Or, that the much promised trip to the zoo is impossible as you can't walk?

The guilt is immense.

The guilt is not improved by media constructions of the 'good mother'. How many news articles are written about children watching too much television or spending too much time on an iPad? Television fetes mothers who bake cupcakes, run marathons, and volunteer for the PTA. When they only thing you are capable of on a bad day is making a packed lunch, the myth of the SuperMom feels like an extra massive kick in the teeth. To be a mother with fibromyalgia is to be a failure.

Feminist Mothering with Fibromyalgia

I'm writing this for Fibromyalgia Awareness Day and I'm having a relatively good day. I have time for a nap before collecting my daughter from school and I managed to get some work done. I've balanced the need to pay my rent with caring for my child. Most days aren't this good and, even if they were, it wouldn't change the stigma of being a disabled mother. Or, erase the guilt for not being a great mother.

In child protection, the term 'good enough mothering' is used to describe women with multiple support needs who have children—whether these needs involve substance use, alcohol dependency, mental illness or trauma. This is what mothering with fibromyalgia is: good enough mothering. It's just not that easy to remember this when faced with a disappointed child who only wanted to visit the zoo.

Room For Our Escape

Hollywood's Woman Problem in Action Films by Christina Paschyn

Everyone wants to feel like a badass once in a while, and for most people the only way they can is by zoning out in front of a big screen and losing themselves in a spy or gangster shoot 'em up film. But here's a little known fact: it's not just men watching these flicks. Women love action films, too. It's a lie that we would rather watch rom-coms instead.

At least, I know I certainly did when I was growing up. I devoured films like the Batman franchise, Indiana Jones and Star Wars up until college when my interest began to wane. Guess why.

Because it was then when I finally realized these films weren't being made for me and Hollywood couldn't give a crap about what women want to see in their action heroes. For the longest time, probably since the age of five, I always identified with the male lead of these films. In reality most women do too. Seriously, what woman really goes into a film fantasizing that she too can be a passive damsel in distress or another bloody female victim? It's banal. Women want adventures too, and we want to feel that crazy adrenaline rush that only comes when you see the hero beating up someone who deserves it.

Unfortunately, it's always a hero and very rarely a heroine who gets to pull that stunt off. And that's why so many women stop going to see action films like James Bond, Superman, Men in Black, gangster films and even the upcoming zombie apocalypse film World War Z. It's extremely frustrating to see yourself and all women portrayed as sex objects, love interests or helpmates over and over again. We're rarely, if ever, the main character and the female character's personal goals always seem to be centered around getting the hero to rescue and fall in love with her. It gets old.

Don't think negative and passive portrayals of women in action films are that pervasive? Think again—they're pervasive in Hollywood films in general, even in children's cartoons.

According to the Women's Media Center, in 2011 women accounted for only 11% of all film protagonists. This means the vast majority of female characters are depicted in supporting roles—in other words, they're there to look pretty or help the male main character achieve his goals. Female characters are less likely to be shown in positions of power or leadership roles.[1]

---

[1] Women's Media Center, 2012, p.42.

Women are underrepresented in general on the silver screen. They comprised only 33% of all characters in the top-grossing films of 2011,[2] and in G-rated family films boy characters outnumber girl characters three to one.[3]

Women are sexually objectified in the movies, too. Even young girls. Female characters continue to show dramatically more skin than their male counterparts, and feature extremely tiny waists and other exaggerated body characteristics. This hypersexualization and objectification of female characters leads to unrealistic body ideals in very young children, cementing and often reinforcing negative body images and perceptions during the formative years. Research shows that lookism still pervades cinematic content in very meaningful ways.

The real-life negative consequences of Hollywood's portrayal of women are shocking. Girls as young as six are beginning to view themselves as sex objects.[4] And even five-year-olds hold negative body images about themselves.[5] Meanwhile, boys are also being socialized to view women as inferior and subordinate sex objects in men's lives.

Still don't believe the movies treat women that badly? Let's take a look at some recently released adult and children's action films.

World War Z

OK, I haven't seen this yet, but I'm not sure I want to. Early reviews of the film say Brad Pitt plays an ex-UN official who saves the world from a zombie apocalypse while his wife hides in a naval carrier with their kids. Wow, that's different.

By the way, I think apocalypse filmmakers need a lesson in originality. Why do they all use the same hero dad/passive mom trope? Just take a look at Independence Day—it's the men who fly the big planes in this one. Will Smith's stripper girlfriend and the president's wife just kind of sit around in places far away from the action. Meanwhile, an alcoholic dead-beat dad gets to redeem himself by sacrificing his life to blow up the alien spaceship. Then there's the remake of War of the Worlds, starring Tom Cruise, and 2012 with John Cusack. Both feature divorced dads who reconfirm their manhood in the eyes of their ex-wives by saving their kids. Indeed, in most of

---

[2] Women's Media Center, 2012, p42.
[3] Geena Davis Institute on Gender in Media.
[4] Women's Media Center 2012, p.43.
[5] Wood, 2012.

these films the dads have either just gotten divorced or are struggling to 'find' themselves (At the start of the film, Brad Pitt's character in World War Z is a stay-at-home dad and apparently hates it). As Alyssa Rosenberg argues in Slate, what better way for these guys to reassert their masculinity than by saving the world while their "empowered" wives sit scared at home?

Hansel & Gretel: Witch Hunters

This has to be one of the most sexist movies of the year, which was so disappointing. Before I sat down to watch the film in its entirety, I had watched clips of it off a person's screen in a plane seat two rows in front of me. Without any sound, the movie looked pretty cool and it seemed the female lead, Gretel, had an exciting storyline. Unfortunately, I soon discovered the movie is a lot better without the dialogue. Here's the premise: Both Hansel and Gretel are supposed to be badass witch hunters and they go around killing primarily female evildoers. Now, my problem with the film isn't that all of the evil witches are women. I actually give the film props for sticking with the traditional understanding of a witch. And anyway, the massacre scenes are so stylized and outrageous (we're talking explosions and trolls popping people's heads off with their gigantic feet) it's just humorous to watch. Besides, plenty of crappy men end up getting brutally killed off, too.

No, the sexism lies in how the film treats Gretel. Apparently she possesses some sort of special "white witch" power, which is why the evil witches want to capture and kill her later on in the film. She is also the one who, as a child, saved her chubby brother's butt when he was about to get eaten by the gingerbread house witch. Yet despite all this, guess who the real hero of the movie is? That's right, Hansel. Gretel, on the other hand, keeps getting beaten up by men (much worse than Hansel ever is) and is very nearly raped. But lucky for her, she gets rescued by some random troll who really doesn't even belong in the film. And for someone who apparently has special powers, she never gets to use them to her advantage.

I guess her specialness isn't all that important either, because guess who gets to narrate the film? Not Gretel, that's for sure. It's apparent the tables have turned since they were kids and Hansel is the real witch killer now. Did I tell you how disappointed I was with this film? I thought it looked so good, but I was so wrong.

Women are also heavily sexualized for the male gaze in this film. Hansel gets to have sex with a hot good witch. Now, on the plane, this scene looked pretty sexy. It starts off with Hansel standing around with his shirt off and, believe me, he looks pretty good. Then the good witch gets naked, but it's tasteful because we never see her bits, and then they jump into the hot "healing" waters for some wet fun. But silly me, I forgot they edit out nudity for plane screens. In the uncensored version, the witch gets fully naked in front of the camera (her breasts and posterior are exposed for the viewers). Suddenly Hansel's shirtless scene isn't all it's cracked up to be.

And then there's Gretel, who doesn't get to show any sort of a sexual appetite of her own. But don't worry. Lots of men get to ogle her instead! At one point a peasant boy (another pointless character) feels up her breasts while she's unconscious. That's a perfectly normal thing for a boy to do, right? Not rapey at all. But hey, it all works out in the end because Gretel wakes up, grabs the horny teen's hand and gives him a dirty look. That makes everything alright. There's also a tavern scene where a guy's body explodes and the blood lands on everyone in the room, but mostly on Gretel who is front and center. We see the blood splashing all over her face. It's as subtle as a "cum" shot in porn.

Lastly, there's the added problem that everyone keeps calling each other "bitch" in the film. Hansel and Gretel call the witches bitches, the witches call themselves bitches and the men who try to rape Gretel call her a bitch, too. It's funny at first but then the underlying misogyny starts to get to you. And by the way Hollywood filmmakers, enough with the attempted rape scenes. Do you think it's somehow empowering for women to see a female character almost get raped? It doesn't matter if she escapes the rape on her own or if someone else helps her. All it says is, "Hey ladies, don't get too uppity because if you do someone will try to rape you!" Regardless whether the rape is carried through or not, we get your intention. It's to put women back in their place.

Escape from Planet Earth

This children's cartoon was so obnoxious and aggravating that I had to walk away a half hour into the film. But I read a recap of the rest of the film, courtesy of Reel Girl, and surprise! It ended just the way I thought it would. The movie is about two brothers, one weak and nerdy and one brawny but dumb, and their age-old sibling rivalry over who is the real hero of their space missions. To make a long story short, the brothers go on an alien adventure to the planet Earth, and the nerdier brother's young son gets to tag along as well. But here's the best part: there's a sub-plot about the womanly rivalry between the nerdy brother's supportive stay-at-home wife (who valiantly gave up her own space career to raise her son) and the female commander of the space mission. Guess how the latter is portrayed? She's an insecure career woman who is willing to put her crew in jeopardy to win the love of some evil space captain. Take that, feminist movement! By the way, the housewife doesn't get to go on the intergalactic adventure. She stays at home while her son and husband have fun.

I read a review of the film that said it was pretty good on "girl power." How much do you want to bet that a man wrote that article? Honestly, this movie left me flabbergasted. Is this really what passes as female empowerment in Hollywood? Pitting women with different life goals against each other in cat fights? I just couldn't believe this movie was made during the 21st century. What the hell does Hollywood think it's teaching boys and girls about proper gender roles? This, ladies and gentlemen, is the patriarchy personified in a children's cartoon.

So why do shitty movies like these keep getting made? One reason is that women continue to hit a glass ceiling in the film industry. According to the Geena Davis institute on Gender in Media, only 7% of directors, 20% of producers and 13% of writers in the entertainment industry are women. And unfortunately, the lack of women behind the camera directly correlates with how women are represented in front of it.

With such a dearth of female representation in front of and behind the camera, it's a struggle to champion female stories and voices. The Institute's research proves that female involvement in the creative process is imperative for creating greater gender balance before production even begins. There is a causal relationship between positive female portrayals and female content creators involved in production. In fact, when even one woman writer works on a film, there is a 10.4% difference in screen time for female characters. Sadly, men outnumber women in key production roles by nearly 5 to 1.

Movie execs also keep feeding us the lie that men and women and boys and girls won't see films with strong female main characters. So instead they cater their films to teenage boys and men, whom they believe will spend more money at the box office. But they're wrong. Women buy more than half of cinema tickets. That means more women than men are going to see films. And did you know that, when controlled for budget, films with female protagonists make just as much money as films with male protagonists? Meanwhile, movies with larger budgets make more money regardless of which sex is playing the main character.[6]

---

[6] Women's Media Center, 2012, p.10.

So maybe, just maybe, if Hollywood gave us an action film with a strong female main character, both men AND women would happily see it.

Instead, they give us crap like Kick-Ass 2. This film features a butt-kicking 15-year-old female superhero. So far so good, right? Then she goes and says something stupid like, "Take Out Your Tampon," to her male colleague. Because women trashing their own sex is sooo funny, right? In the first film, she also got to call bad guys "cunts". What's the problem with that? Well, while Hit Girl may be a tough woman she doesn't personify female empowerment. She chooses to ridicule women instead. I've seen this recently in quite a few films and TV shows. The writers think it's funny to have a female character emasculate her male friend by calling him out on his "femininity"—in other words, his weaknesses. And that's the problem. As Jezebel correctly points out, even in films featuring strong female characters, even those characters equate womanhood with weakness.

Maybe these characters think they are the exception to the rule. Or maybe they think if they criticize other women enough, they might be accepted as "one of the guys." They hope to climb the ranks of the patriarchy by trying to fit in with it. Too bad by mocking their own sex, they're only degrading themselves as well (Faludi, 1991).

All of this goes to show action films are being written by men for men. And, unfortunately, real women are being left out of the conversation.

As Geena Davis said, women deserve to get an adrenaline rush from action films too:

> "Thelma and Louise had a big reaction, there was a huge thing at the time, that, 'Oh my god, these women had guns and they actually killed a guy!' … That movie made me realize—you can talk about it all you want, but watch it with an audience and talk to women who have seen this movie and they go, 'YES!' They feel so adrenalized and so powerful after seeing some women kick some ass and take control of their own fate. … Women go, 'Yeah—fucking right!' Women don't get to have that experience in the movies. But hey, people go to action movies for a reason; they want to feel adrenalized and they want to identify with the hero, and if only guys get to do that then it's crazy."[7]

The Ms. Magazine blog post, where the above quotation is featured, also makes some valid points about current action heroines' bodies. Far too few of them have any real muscle on their

---

[7] Derr, 2013.

womanly frames. Instead the stars who play them resort to extreme weight loss diets to ensure they will look good in skin-tight cat suits (like, as the article says, Anne Hathaway did for the latest Batman installment). That's fine if your goal is to be thin, and the author does a good job not to body shame the skinny stars who play these roles. But much has been said of the fact that Hollywood promotes unrealistic body ideals for women. Right now, thin and waif-like is in. But really, how effective is that physique for beating up bad guys?

As Jean Kilbourne writes in her 1999 essay "The More You Subtract, the More You Add," Hollywood and American media keep trying to "cut women down to size."

> "'We cut Judy down to size,' says an ad for a health club. 'Soon, you'll both be taking up less space,' says an ad for a collapsible treadmill, referring both to the product and to the young woman exercising on it. The obsession with thinness is most deeply about cutting girls and women down to size. It is only a symbol, albeit a very powerful and destructive one, of tremendous fear of female power. Powerful women are seen by many people (women as well as men) as inherently destructive and dangerous. Some argue that it's men's awareness of just how powerful women can be that has created the attempts to keep women small. Indeed, thinness as an ideal has always accompanied periods of greater freedom for women—as soon as we got the vote, boyish flapper bodies came into vogue. No wonder there is such pressure on young women today to be thin, to shrink, to be like little girls, not to take up too much space, literally or figuratively."[8]

Is this what is happening in Hollywood action films? Can strong female heroines be shown only if they are too frail to pull off any of the stunts in real life?

Male fear of powerful women is probably the reason why in many platonic pairings of male and female action heroes, the woman rarely gets to exhibit any sexual agency of her own. "The emphasis for girls and women is always on being desirable, not on experiencing desire," Kilbourne writes. So no wonder Gretel's only sexual experience in the film is getting felt up by a perverted peasant boy. Meanwhile, Hansel gets to have sex without being dangled as eye candy for viewers, unlike his sexual partner. Spoiler alert, she ends up dying at the end of the film. I guess that's her punishment for showing any sexual interest at all.

---

[8] Kilbourne, 1999 cited in Kirk and Okazawa-Rey, 2010.

Now, do I think male filmmakers deliberately insert these misogynistic elements into their films? I don't know. Perhaps their own socialization in a patriarchal society has made them blind to the obvious. But the only way things will change for women in Hollywood is if we make some noise.

So my feminist friends, I beg you, please don't spend your money on crappy films that propagate negative stereotypes about women. Don't see an action film where it's clear the female lead is just there as eye candy. You're just encouraging men to view women as vapid sex objects. And whether you want to believe it or not, these films subtly promote violence against you. And they're trying to keep all women down.

Why not see a movie made by a woman instead? Then go write a gushing review about it and pass it along on the internet.

BIBLIOGRAPHY

Derr, H., 2013. Where Have You Gone, Sarah Connor? *MS. Magazine*, [online] Available at: http://msmagazine.com/blog/2013/06/11/where-have-you-gone-sarah-connor/.

Faludi, S., 1991. *Backlash: The Undeclared War Against American Women*. New York: Broadway Books.

Geena Davis Institute on Gender in Media, [online] Available at: http://www.seejane.org/research/.

Kirk, G. and Okazawa-Rey, M., 2010. *Women's Lives: Multicultural Perspectives*. New York: McGraw Hill Higher Education.

Magowan, M., 2013. 'Escape From Planet Earth' humiliates working woman. *Reel Girl*, [online] Available at: http://reelgirl.com/2013/03/escape-from-planet-earth-humilaites-working-woman/.

Rosenberg, A., 2013. Brad Pitt Wins the Zombie War, Loses the Daddy Wars in World War Z. *Slate*, [online] Available at: http://www.slate.com/blogs/xx_factor/2013/06/21/brad_pitt_s_world_war_z_has_some_very_retro_gender_politics.html.

Stewart, D., 2013. Hit Girl to Dude in Kick-Ass 2: 'Take Your Tampon Out'. *Jezebel*, [online] Available at: http://jezebel.com/hit-girl-to-dude-in-kick-ass-2-take-your-tampon-out-514264289.

Women's Media Center, 2012. *The Status of Women in the U.S. Media*, [online] Available at: http://www.womensmediacenter.com/page/-/media%20relations/WMC%20Status%20of%20Women%20in%20US%20Media%202012.pdf.

Wood, J. T., 2012. *Gendered Lives: Communication, Gender, & Culture*. Boston, MA: Wadsworth.

Room For Our Future

What's in a Word? by Millie Slavidou

There are many examples on the internet and elsewhere, especially in feminist literature, of *woman* being spelt in alternative ways, such as *womon*, *womyn*, etc. I am not here to analyse such usages: I neither condone nor condemn; rather I simply observe their existence.

Let's concentrate on the word *woman*. What is its story? Where does it come from?

I have seen some peculiar claims circulating on the internet (and let's face it, there is a lot of nonsense on the internet) that 'woman' either derives from 'womb-man' or that it is 'woman-man'. As folk etymology goes, the former is frankly laughable, and the latter is a more understandable mistake, but one that conflates the modern word 'man' with the Old English word *man* and assumes that the meaning is the same.

Womb-man takes no account of anything other than the similarity of 'womb' in its modern form to the modern form of *woman*, or at least the first syllable of the word. But as we shall see, the first syllable did not start off that way.

The modern word with the /o/ sound, or the shwa, in the singular, developed during the **Middle English** period. Prior to that, it was /i/, the vowel that is preserved in the plural, in pronunciation if not in spelling. It comes from **Old English**, which is how we refer to the language as it was spoken before 1100, and from the time when it first began to be written down. To give some perspective, the language used by King Alfred (he of the burning cakes legend) would have been Old English.

Returning to our word, *woman* was in Old English generally known as *wifman* and is made up of two elements: *wif* and *man*. The first part, *wif*, meant 'female', and the second meant, not 'man' in the sense of 'male human being' that we have today, but 'person, human', and was used equally for both sexes.

Before you start wondering about the default male in times of yore, it should be noted that this is not comparable with some modern usages of 'man', where people wish it to refer to both women and men. There was in fact another form in Old English that meant 'male person', and that was *wer*. This form could sometimes also be teamed up with the gender neutral *man*; *wer-man*, in much the same way as *wifman*. The male form was lost over time, with only a last remnant of it still to be found in 'werewolf', but *wifman* remained and gradually developed to become *woman*.

So let's go back to the word as it was and examine the first element; where did wif come from? Well, it is **Germanic**, and to help us attest to this fact, we can see a cognate in modern **German** Weib. A cognate is a word which is related, which comes from the same root as another. Think of it as the linguistic equivalent of a cousin, which may be close or distant. Returning now to Weib, this is a German cognate of wif signifying 'woman, female'. Both of these come from **Proto-Germanic** *wībam*, meaning 'woman'.

So far, so good. But it is hard to trace it any further; its origins from there further back in time are obscure. The two main theories are that it could be from **Proto-Indo-European** root *weip-*, meaning 'twist, wrap', through the idea of 'veiled person', or from *ghwibh-*, a root meaning 'shame' or 'pudenda'.

There seem to be several problems with these theories. Firstly, looking at *weip-*, there is no reason to suppose that the speakers of the Proto-Indo-European language veiled women, nothing to associate this root with women in particular, other than later prejudices and preconceptions being applied to an earlier time. Indeed, all archaeological evidence points to the contrary. Early art depicting women has not shown them to be veiled at all, and in fact there is no evidence at all to suggest that women in Proto-Indo-European cultures were covered until after these words were established in their meaning as 'woman', which would post-date any connection between the meanings 'wrap/ conceal/ cover' and 'woman', thereby undermining this theory.

In the second instance, there are only two proposed derivatives of *ghwibh-*; the Germanic root signifying 'woman' and a word from **Tocharian**, an extinct language known only from manuscripts discovered in China. The proposed word in Tocharian is *kip*, meaning 'female pudenda'. Although it is possible that *kip* and *wif* are related in meaning 'female', it seems to me quite a stretch of imagination to assume that 'woman' and 'pudenda' must have derived from a word meaning 'shame'; again, I believe that this is later prejudice being applied retrospectively. Where is the archaeological evidence supporting women in positions of shame? The artwork, the ornaments, or indeed the tales from early mythology of Indo-European peoples? There is nothing to link 'woman' with 'shame'. However, this is not to say that the Tocharian and Germanic words are unrelated; simply that the proposed meaning is problematic.

What's in a Word?

There are no cognates in other languages meaning anything similar, no other linguistic evidence to point to this meaning, and in none of the proposed derivatives are there clear overtones of shame. And as for it meaning 'pudenda', again, there is only the one example of this word. Equally, both the Tocharian and Germanic words could have developed from a root meaning 'female'; it could be the Tocharian that diverged rather than the Germanic, or indeed both could come from a different root entirely. The Tocharian is the only link to pudenda, and there is no compelling reason to suppose that this was the original meaning of the Germanic root too. Indeed, the only point of common reference for the two words is *female*.

Going back once more to our **Old English** word, *wif*, it is not hard to see the other modern cognate; *wife*. This evolved from meaning more generally 'woman' and became more specific as 'female spouse', possibly through its link with the Old English verb *gewifian*. This meant 'to take a wife'. It is not to be confused with 'marry', as obviously this is a word that may be applied to both genders, whereas the original sense of *gewifian* was for a man to take a wife. For the woman, on the contrary, there was another verb, *weddian*, which developed into the modern 'wed', and meant 'promise, pledge' and ultimately, 'marry'.

Mother's Lament by Susan Dunford

Oh give to me my daughter, give to me my child. My one, poor one, my poor and loving child. Do not leave me to beg at my master's door, but take pity on me and show me where I should look. Where should I search for that which I have lost? And the loss is more than I can bear.

You tell me to return another day, that there may be answers then. So I return, return, and turn and turn. My life has become a circle of symmetry. You leave me walking in circles, declaring me crazy. Everyone looks at the crazy woman walking in circles, talking to herself. For who will listen? No matter how loud my voice, it will not be heard. All that I can do is to walk in circles. And as I turn and turn I have nothing but symmetry when it is sympathy that I require.

Do not turn me away! Do not deny me! Do not deny yourself, your faults, your thoughts and actions. You deny and deny, and lie and lie. Give me my daughter. Give her to me now. Don't give me your lies. Don't deny what you have done. I walk this circle, walk this circle, walk this circle, and you keep saying the same filthy lies. The dust sticks to my shoes, I sweat as I walk, but it is you who is dirty. You and your stinking, rotten lies. Go on then, deny it. Pretend you didn't see her. Pretend you didn't take her. Hate her. Rape her. Kill her. Give me my daughter. Tell me what you did and give her to me now. Give me her body. Give her back to me. You call me a mad mother, but without my daughter I am no mother at all. You give me a label and deny me even that. She is mine, born from me and of me and part of me. You have taken part of me, no wonder I am crazy. You have taken my mind along with her body.

Give me my daughter. Give her back now. I want her five-year-old body pressing against me, sobbing over a scraped knee. I want her teenage self angry against injustice. I want her adult laugh, talking with friends from college. I want to see her children. I want to see her grow older, live beyond my time. I want her sitting by the radio, listening to songs from her youth. I want to see her live her life to its natural end. I want her to have a life, opportunity. I want her. Give her to me now.

I will not quietly go away. I will not slink into the night and pretend to adjust, accept the facts, and live around the shape that she has left in the world. You think that by stealing her away, sneaking in like a thief, I will not notice. That people will turn their heads, pretend she was never there. That isn't how it works. When you disappear a person, you create a black hole of absence. You create a force which will destroy you. She will achieve more with her disappearance than she ever did with her appearance. The black hole of her existence will bring power and death. It will bend light out of shape, suck the universe towards it, until the whole earth is looking and looking, staring into the depth of her non-existence. The lack of her will be more noticeable than the presence of her. You have created the black hole which will destroy you, and even if you give her back you will be sucked into the emptiness, the nothingness, which you wanted to create.

Give me back my daughter. There will be no forgiveness for you, for what you have done can never be forgiven. Give me back my daughter. Give back my daughter. Giv bak m d.ter. Give her back. Give back. You try to create a nation by destroying the nation. Give back my daughter. You create nothing but your own destruction.

I despise you. I spit on you. I pray you have no coffin, no burial, no resting place. Give me back my daughter and we will tear you apart, tear off your limbs, rip off your eyelids. Smile at the sweet sound of your screams and dance over your body. My daughter has no body but I demand that you give her back to me now. There is nowhere left for me to go. I will not move, I will not leave. If you try to make me move I will circle back to you, swear at you and spit at you. You took my everything from me and now you must give her back. Fury envelopes me, inhabits me, rises from me and I send her screaming towards you. I grow and become misshapen, distorted, a behemoth. I am a giant of fury, a fury of vengeance. Give back the daughter. I am no mother. I have come to claim the daughter. Fury claims the daughter and without the daughter there is only Fury. Vengeance and Fury and Death, for ever and ever, Amen.

An Open Letter to Our Immigrant Parents by Priscilla Lugo

Two weeks ago, after I published an article with Latinas4Change, I sent the link to my family for them to read it. Later on, my dad, an immigrant who doesn't know much English, told me, "Cada ves que mandas algo, lo tengo que leer dos o tres veces para poder entenderlo. Pero quiero que sepas que estoy tan orgulloso de ti."

After he told me this, my heart broke. I know Spanish because I come from a house where Spanish is pretty much all that is spoken, but once I started going to school, I dropped it and started speaking more English. I became more fluent in English than I ever was in Spanish, and I knew that because of this I always struggled to communicate as well with my dad than with my mom (who speaks fluent English). But I was just now realizing how much of a difference it made to him, how much of an effort he had to put in just to understand me. I was just seeing how difficult it must have been for him to say, "No mas dilo en ingles para que sera mas facil para ti" when I should have been the one making it easier for him.

So here is an open letter to our immigrant parents who worked so hard and sacrificed so much for us just to have a better opportunity than they ever did. To my parents, but especially my dad for being the man I've always needed in my life, and the only one I can ever count on. Gracias, papi. Te quiero mucho.

Para Mis Padres,

Gracias por siempre estar a mi lado y por siempre apoyarme y protejerme.

Gracias for nunca dejarme olvidar mi cultura y gracias por no dejarme olvidar de donde vengo.

Gracias por crear una persona inteligente, fuerte, y independiente.

Gracias por siempre poner mis sueños primero y por siempre poner mis hermanos y yo primero.

Nunca voy a saber todo lo que han sacrificado, pero gracias por eso tabien.

Ya se que no podría ser fácil dejar todos tus sueños para asegurarte que mis hermanos y yo podríamos tener todo lo que queríamos y necesitábamos.

An Open Letter to Our Immigrant Parents

Quiero que sepan que la mission de mi vida es ser una hija que merece tener padres tan increibles como ustedes. Yo se que por sus sacrificios, amor y apoyo eterno, puedo ayudar a cambiar el mundo. Y nada de esto sería posible sin ustedes.

Los quiero tanto,

Tu hija.

Being Chicana in College by Priscilla Lugo

Despite what everyone told me about applying to college and being in college, nothing could have prepared me for what awaited me as I began the long and strenuous process that was college.

Applying to college was different for me than it was for most people. I am a first generation Chicana who wasn't entirely sure what she was getting into. My parents were extremely encouraging and stood by me 100% of the time, some people from my community however, were not. I was constantly being undermined in my college decision and being told "Pero eres niña buena! You come from a good family, you're smart; you can just marry some guy and be someone's trophy wife." Things like this haunted my thoughts and almost scared me into submission of this stereotype that seemed to follow me everywhere I went. They talked about being a trophy wife or a stay at home mom as if that was the greatest thing I could ever achieve. It scared me, but I persevered and went big on all my choices and didn't let anything hold me back from dreaming big, and soon enough I heard back and I made one of the greatest decisions of my life and chose to spend the next 4 years of my life at The University of Texas at Austin.

College life was definitely an adjustment. I had to prepare myself to keep up academically and to be surrounded by all the different people around me. Despite UT Austin being a diverse campus, I was still one of the only women of color in all of my classes, and usually the only Latina. I was at times overlooked in my classes with my white professors and I felt the need to prove myself so I often worked twice as hard just to make sure I felt heard and noticed, despite being shy in the classroom. It wasn't until I sat down with one of my professors who was also a Latina and in her last year of graduate school. I told her my aspirations in life and how at times I knew that I was being overlooked, and she had a sincere talk with me about how she, too, went back to school because she knew if she wanted to be taken seriously in her field, she had to get her Ph.D. She worked in the non-profit world and was a part of the team that gathered information to help legislators write bills to help minorities living in the California area. She left her job because she, too, was being overlooked and knew the only way to advance and to ensure that it would no longer happen would be if she had the title "Dr." before her name. After that, I knew that no matter what, I had to continue my education because I wouldn't give anyone an excuse to overlook me.

Being Chicana in College

Outside of the classroom I also faced some adversity that I didn't realize I needed to overcome. Two blocks from my dorm is the most racist fraternity on campus that under their rules it explicitly says, "No interracial dating" as well as "No Mexicans." I've seen some of these frat boys on campus and I hear them talking about how fine Selena Gomez is; so they're willing to sexualize us, just not date us, be seen with us, or let us into their house/parties.

Being Chicana in college is nothing like I expected it to be. Stereotypes surround me everywhere I go and seem to be all people see in me when they meet me. People see what they want to see in me, and whenever they do see something good in me, they count on me to represent my entire culture and people. But I realized it's up to me if I let it get to me—it's up to me if I prosper despite everything that is holding me back, and I will prosper.

Love Sick by Erika Garrett

Can I just say, before I go on and on in this piece, I am not a psychiatrist nor have I ever studied human psychology. This is a meditation on my own lived experiences.

We use the term 'love sick' to describe that odd and sometimes unsettling feeling when we first start dating someone that we really like. The butterflies in the stomach on the first few dates, the daydreaming, the hoping and the waiting. None of this is a bad thing or an indication that there is something not quite right going on. I'm talking about the absence of any appetite, stomach churning worry, paranoia and a sense of being utterly overwhelmed by what has happened.

Unfortunately, I have quite the collection of failed and abusive relationships lingering around in my past, like a bad smell that refuses to go away. In all of those I had the so-called classic symptoms of being love sick. I have been known to eat so poorly that I lost a stone in weight and was reduced to a shattered heap of woman. That's just not healthy or sustainable.

There seems to be this acceptance that when we meet someone that we are really attracted to and want to be with night and day, that losing weight and clinging for dear life to our mobile phones is entirely acceptable. People will tell you that you are 'love sick' and that it will pass. I'm embarrassed to admit to doing an internet search to find out if how I was feeling was normal, turned out that it was. In hindsight, I should have listened to what my body, my very soul was telling me—something isn't right.

I think it is indicative of the 'if he hits you, he likes you' narrative that girls are fed when they start school and mix with boys. It makes abuse seem like an inevitable consequence of someone being madly in love with you. As girls, we are conditioned by society to accept that we have to put up with actions and words that upset us as that is our place in life. The lie of being love sick is to take away the alarm bells of abuse and see it as a positive sign that we are falling in love so hard that our body cannot cope with it.

It would be dangerous for me to say that the 'right' person wouldn't keep you waiting for a text or talk about his exes. Abusive men are very clever in how they secure your full attention, they will gauge what they can get away with. There are clues that I missed or glossed over, though. I am not to blame for my abuse but I know now that my body's reaction to a new relationship should always be listened to (even now, I'm still not sure that I trust myself to listen to my

Love Sick

instincts). Abusive men are so subtle in the way that they increase your dependency on them, making you feel like shit is one of them.

Room For Our Knowledge

I am not your Mami by Priscilla Lugo

The majority of women, if not all women, experience some form of sexual harassment, and this stems from society hyper-sexualizing women and our bodies, but Latinas are hyper-sexualized in a way that for the most part, only women of color can relate to.

Latinas are seen as hypersexual beings that live to play out men's weird fantasies. We are seen as subhuman women who only seek out to "trap" men into having their kids while they clinch them for 18 years into giving child support. We are seen as baby mommas, not mothers. We are seen as hypersexual beings rather than just a woman with a regular sexual appetite. We are seen as women who are not capable of being their own person rather than an independent person and human being.

These stereotypes of hyper-sexualizing were made worse when Joe Bovino published his second sexist-trash novel, *Chicaspotting: A Field Guide to Latinas of the United States*, his sequel to *A Field Guide to Chicks of The United States*.[9] Given that Mr. Bovino's trash book has not nor has it made national headlines (although I'm sure he wishes it would), the mere publication of such a book says a lot about our culture and who we are as a society. Now, before you go and look for this book, let me sum it up for you, he utilizes his 93 pages as a way to stereotype all different kinds of Latina women in 14 categories:

1) The Taco Belle (Mexican American);

2) Bumbshell (Brazalian American);

3) Euro-Mina (Argentine American);

4) Trifect (Venezuelan American);

5) Symmetrical Force (Colombian American);

6) Transformer (Cuban American);

7) Ecuadorable (Ecuadorian American);

8) La Guitarra (Puerto Rican – South);

---

[9] Bovino, Joe. (2015). *ChicaSpotting: A Field Guide to Latinas of the United States*. Saoirse Publishing LLC.

9) Nuyorican (Puerto Rican – Northeast);

10) Cinnamon Swirl (Dominican American – Florida);

11) Beauty Call (Dominican American – Northeast);

12) Perusian (Peruvian American);

13) Pupusa (Salvadoran American); and

14) Hotemalan (Guatemalan American).

He then continues to rate these "species" of women according to their appearance, as well as factors based on their behaviors like friendliness, neuroticism, nesting, maintenance, superficiality, and promiscuity—all of which have their own corresponding emoji to help rate these "species." He then elaborates on how you can spot these women and how you can cross-reference them in relation to his first book, *A Field Guide to Chicks of The United States.*

Now, please let me take a moment before I vomit describing what he does next. Okay, I'm ready. When he actually goes into detail to describe these "species" of Latina women he utilizes horrible stereotypes and diction. He describes "The Taco Belle" as having a "dusky complexion" as well as "out of shape because exercise is less emphasized in Mexican culture." And just when I thought Mr. Bovino couldn't be any more of a sexist pig, he then describes the lovely "Sara Ramirez, Grey's Anatomy actress as a 'Taco Belle'." While Sara Ramirez has previously said that she loves her body and "know[s] [her] boyfriend loves to have something to hold onto" he still pits this incredible woman, activist, and humanitarian against another fellow "Taco Belle," Eva Longoria, saying that while it may be true that some men like having a little more to hold onto, "Eva Longoria shows how hot a Taco Belle can be if she exercises regularly." Not only is he being sexist, by putting two women up against each other, he is undermining one woman and her body and taking away every good thing she has ever done for the world and summing her up as a derogatory "species" that is less than another woman because of her body.

I wish I could continue on to describe the rest of the horrible things he does throughout the rest of his book, but honestly, my head hurts just summing it up. While Joe Bovino is not to blame for society sexualizing Latinas in this way, he is a (huge) part of the problem. By publishing this book, he further normalized the concept of sexualizing Latinas. He and his book make it okay to call Latinas "spicy" or "saucy" or any other word that we may be called.

I am not your Mami

I know what it's like to be hyper-sexualized by men. To be catcalled on the streets and have men yell vulgar things at you while you fear for your life. I know what it's like to have someone at a bar or club come up to you and say, "Hey, Mami, how are you doing tonight?" and feel as if you're the one who did something wrong or dirty. It's taken me a long time to realize that it's not me. I'm not dressing a certain way. I'm not acting in a particular way. It's not me. It's society that has brought up men to think that it's okay to do this to women, to catcall and to harass them on the streets, in a bar, or at work. They have normalized this form of harassment to the point where 81% of women have experienced some form of street harassment. They have done this and they've done it with the help of Joe Bovino and all others who make jokes of Latinas and all women of color. They have normalized this experience.

As a Latina, as a Chicana, as a "Taco Belle," I am telling you not to let the Joe Bovinos of the world, the catcallers, and the street harassers get to you. You are not someone that can be categorized into a "simple species" or "common name." You are all complex, incredible, and independent women capable of changing the world—capable of changing the way society sees us. So I'm here telling you to take back the word Latina and make it your own. Have it mean something different for you.

And finally, to all the Joe Bovinos, catcallers, street harassers:

I will not let you define me, and

I am not your "mami," and no, I won't call you "papi."

Understanding Feminist Standpoints: Situated Knowledges of Gender, Race, and Class Inequality by Egoyibo Okoro

> "[Feminism is] a struggle against the very existence of power, a struggle for a mode of organization and life which would no longer be maintained by the distinctions of class and power." (Braidotti, 1991, p.157)

> "It is axiomatic that if we don't define ourselves for ourselves, we will be defined by others—for their use and to our detriment." (Collins, 1991, p.26)

> "The mind of the man and the mind of the woman is the same, but this business of living makes women use their minds in ways that men don't even have to think about." (Collins, 1991, p.25)

Historically, the identity of "woman" has always been in question. She is human, yet humanity is man. Pondering this anomaly, Simone de Beauvoir asked:

> "what is a woman?", and some people answered and many still answer: "she is a womb"—A baby-making machine, whose worth is linked to her (in)ability to reproduce and increase the human population. From culture to culture, civilized and otherwise, woman has for a long time been under the influence of patriarchy (read male dominance): shed of her intelligence, infantilized, manipulated and directed—as if she were witless—by man to accept whatever identity, roles, obligations, and/or rights he assigns to her. Meekly, she accepts these roles, and sees herself as mother, "good wife" (read submissive, mute), and supporter, but rarely as a person independent of man. So total, so domineering was this domination that, "woman cannot think of herself without man"[10]

so she seeks his validation and directions, and thus acts—as directed—as: the dutiful young woman who must "behave" or she will remain unwed—a cursed state, the clipping of her niece's clitoris to prevent "promiscuity", the "good daughter" who accepts the payment of money (bride price) on her head, and/or the "good wife" who meekly welcomes her husband's second wife because it's his right as a sexually insatiable man. Truly, patriarchy brainwashed woman into submissiveness: told her to play coy because she's more attractive to him that way, defined her femininity as gentle, soft-spoken, weak, child-like and needing man to survive; he then told

---

[10] Beauvoir, 2009.

Understanding Feminist Standpoints:
Situated Knowledges of Gender, Race, and Class Inequality

her— when she objected—that he was being chivalrous. It was these false beliefs of woman's weakness and ordained dependence on man for survival that Sojourner Truth responded to, when she cried:

"Look at me! Look at my arm! I have ploughed, and planted, and gathered into barns, and no man could head me! And ain't I a woman?"

Patriarchy being "a sort of 'metaphysical cannibalism' which feeds upon female energy, intelligence and labour force, in order to sustain the monuments of masculine power" , fed on woman, raped and sucked her dry, and, then devalued her using powerful, regular, patriarchal figures like Village Chiefs, Religious Leaders, Fathers, Husbands, and more popular figures such as Aristotle, Plato, St. Thomas, St. Peter, Freud, etc. Powerful men whose writings, actions and utterances portrayed woman as unequal to man; men who held society in thrall with their authoritative power; men to whom a magnificent number of people listened, and emulated. Succinctly put, "he is the subject; he is the absolute. She is the Other". Woman linked intrinsically to man through biological, familial, economic and cultural ties, and shy of the hostile repercussions of lashing out at the chains that shackled her, could not revolt against male dominance without being called "bitch", "man-hater". "man-wanna-be", "emasculator" or "bitter". Thus, it was not simple for woman to revolt against her assigned "Otherness" without "renouncing all the advantages an alliance with the superior caste confers on [her]". But, revolt she did and still does.

Woman revolts every time she shows disloyalty to civilization. Eve revolted when she refused to obey God's command not to eat the "forbidden fruit" of knowledge; White American women of the South revolted when they refused to be "loyal to the ideology of race and segregation" (Rich, 1979, p.278); ten thousand Nigerian women revolted when they marched bare-breasted along the roads of south-east Nigeria, in protest of heavy taxes and non-participation of women in governance (Aba Women's Riot of 1929); women revolt every time we challenge society's perceptions of womanhood; women revolt every time we pick up our pens to write against sexism, gender inequality, discriminatory cultural norms or gender-based violence; women revolt every time they shun society's expectation of them based on their gender. Women have long been in the business of civil disobedience, they just didn't call it feminism. Like Rowbotham rightly noted, "there is no 'beginning' of feminism in the sense that there is no beginning of defiance in women…Female resistance has taken several historical stages". The woman's struggle for identification and recognition, for the right to equal opportunities, is an aged one— aged because this struggle cannot be accurately traced, timed, dated; it is a struggle that began

Understanding Feminist Standpoints:
Situated Knowledges of Gender, Race, and Class Inequality

when woman started to question the rules of man which he termed "civilization", rules which favored the interests of man, because "those who made and compiled the laws, being men, favored their own sex, and the juriconsults have turned the laws into principles" (de Beauvoir, 2009, p.11). As such, the man (or men) in woman's life should not take it personally if she revolts against these civil laws, but were he (they) to do so—as he(they) more often than not does(do)—woman is justified in wanting to identify herself as one, equal, half of humanity and not a small part (of humanity) that makes up Mankind. The words of Montaigne come to mind: "women are not in the wrong when they decline to accept the rules laid down for them, since the men make these rules without consulting them" (Montaigne, cited in de Beauvoir, 2009, p.11).

Woman having been conditioned to band together with the men in her life—her circle of interaction—did not band together with the other women in her circle, and rarely did she form relationships across racial, cultural, or class lines. So, it is not surprising that when feminist scholarship and activism began, the experiences and viewpoints of colored women were not documented as feminist standpoints. As Lorde rightly noted, "certainly there are very real differences of age, race and sex. But it is not those differences between us that are separating us. It is rather our refusal to recognize those differences, and to examine the distortions which result from our misnaming them and their effects upon human behavior and expectation" (Lorde, 2007, p.115). I think this hesitation (of white women to understand the racial and cultural differences between them and women of color) isn't borne out of spite or any malevolent feelings of superiority; to me, it is borne of white women's lack of understanding of the lives and cultures of colored women; it is borne of the years of stereotyped, negative, identities of Black women (for example) as this and that negatives; it is borne of the differences in white women's and colored women's lives, wherein one group is made up of the daughters of a "superior race" while the other consists of daughters of an "inferior race".

However, this history of differences has to be confronted in order for both sides—black and colored women and white women—to move on towards a greater feminist movement that takes into account every woman's experience and works to better every woman's world irrespective of her race, culture or class. Lorde (2007) urges us to confront this past (of slavery, racism, oppression), because "by ignoring the past we are encouraged to repeat its mistakes… Ignoring the differences of race between women and the implications of those differences presents the most serious threat to the mobilization of women's joint power." (Lorde, 2007, p.117). Disregarding situated viewpoints is a threat to the feminist movement because it is an unjust silencing of viewpoints which is antifeminist, besides the fact that "all silence has a meaning"

Understanding Feminist Standpoints:
Situated Knowledges of Gender, Race, and Class Inequality

(Rich, 1997, p.308). Consequently, the act of not recognizing an individual woman's standpoint means: a silencing of her objections, and the enabling of her oppression. It also means that the white woman regards "women of color as 'Other', the outsider whose experiences and tradition is too 'alien' to comprehend" (Lorde, 2007, p.117). There has to come about a change: in the ways white women perceive women of color, a change in the ways white women respond to racism and the black woman's anger towards racism; there has to be a change, so the feminist movement can grow to achieve more, because "change is growth, and growth can be painful... [But] for Black and white, old and young, lesbian and heterosexual women alike, this can mean new paths to our survival." (Lorde, 2007, p.123). Lorde is also quick to enlighten us on what she means by "change": "when I speak of change I do not mean a simple switch of positions or a lessoning of tensions, nor the ability to smile or feel good. I am speaking of a basic and radical alteration in those assumptions underlying our lives" (Lorde, 2007, p.127).

How do we confront these differences? We—white women and colored women alike—do so by listening to and understanding every woman's experience(s) and situated knowledge(s). We do this by accepting each other's situated knowledge(s), because we need these situated knowledges for "a feminist version of objectivity... [that is] not about transcendence and splitting of subject and object", (Haraway, 1988, p.578, p.583) and because "a culture's best beliefs—what it calls knowledge—are socially situated" (Harding, 1991, p.119). The situated knowledges of Misi Juliette Cummings is a case in point, because hers "is a uniquely individual story, [but] it is as much a collective story, a story of women of her generation, her ethnic and class background, enacting the same versatile sexual behavior." (Wekker, 2006, p.2).

In understanding and accepting individual feminist standpoints, let us bear in mind that disregarding a subjugated minority's point of view is tantamount to oppression, and promotes the single story, and is against the ideals of feminist objectivity. Let us always remember that no woman is free while one is chained, "even when her shackles are very different from [our] own", (Lorde, 2007, pp.132-133).

Understanding Feminist Standpoints:
Situated Knowledges of Gender, Race, and Class Inequality

BIBLIOGRAPHY

Braidotti, R., 1991. *Patterns of Dissonance*. Cambridge: Polity Press.

Collins, P. H., 1991. *Black Feminist Thought: Knowledge, Consciousness, and the Power of Empowerment*. New York: Routledge.

de Beauvoir, S., 2009. *The Second Sex*. New York: Alfred A. Knopf.

Haraway, D., 1988. Situated Knowledges: The Science Question in Feminism and the Privilege of Partial Perspectives *Feminist Studies*, 14(3), pp.575-599.

Harding, S., 1991. *Whose Science? Whose Knowledge?* New York: Cornell University Press.

Lorde, A., 2007. *Sister Outsider: Essays and Speeches*. California: Crossing Press.

Rich, A., 1979. *On Lies, Secrets and Silence: Selected Prose 1966-1978*. New York: W. W. Norton & Company.

The Holy Bible, King James Version. Kerr. W. F, ed., 2000. California: International Publishing.

Wekker, G., 2006. *The Politics of Passion. Women's Sexual Culture in the Afro-Surinamese Diaspora*. New York: Columbia University Press.

Hysteria in Performance: The subversive potential of performative malady
by Effie Samara

> Having a fling with a philosopher also entails safeguarding those components of the mirror that cannot reflect themselves: its backing, its brilliancy, thus its dazzlements, its ecstasies... (Irigaray, 1985, p.151)

Hysteria as a psychosomatic phenomenon, acted or suffered, has been present in discourse from the pre-Socratics onwards, reaching as far back as the Homeric texts and is concomitant with the beginning of the material instantiation of language with all its syntactical implications and epistemic challenges. As a nosological malady, Hysteria bypasses medical symptomatology and serves as a designate for that which is beyond the socially acceptable and the linguistically conceivable. In contemporary philosophy Luce Irigaray, Judith Butler and Julia Kristeva have reinterpreted female intentionality ontologically and linguistically but also in performance through the use of mimesis, hyperbole and contradiction. Hysteria in performance is a powerful weapon combining theatrical mimesis and linguistic and gestural exaggeration, freed from the conventions of limitational grammar. The purpose of this essay is to demonstrate theatre's power to foreground the subversive potential of Hysteria as a tool of empowerment operating both inside and outside the realms of grammatical permissibility and towards the formation of a female syntax.

The impossibility in discourse of the articulation of the *female sex* derives from grammatical limitation: the sex is the property of the subject and as proprietorially predicated the sexualised female, in order to exist in the public or private sphere, is forced to deploy a ready-made code of symbols resulting in a permanent dissonance between intentions and utterances. Her Speech Acts are confined to illogicality or at best, a citational mimicry, an artificed passport to Master Discourse. As an *Other* language, operating outside the codes of traditional syntax, Hysteria, theatrically understood as hyperbole, has become an essentialist weapon against the onslaught of positivist and foundationalist discourse. In theorising Hysteria, linguistic and ontological predication are virtually impossible to separate, given the intimate connection between the notions of Being and Becoming and the questions of Identity, Difference and Predication. In the Irigarean tradition Hysteria is examined through Irigaray's very particular post-Lacanian lens heavily influenced by the metaphysical anxieties in the Platonic dialogues, both of which will be examined here in a little more detail.

Hysteria in Performance: The subversive potential of performative malady

As a medically indefinable malady Hysteria is the performative malady par excellence. In contemporary Anglophone drama Anna Furse's *Augustine* and Sarah Kane's *Cleansed* are both examples of how classically Freudian paradigms deploy a theatrical trope to investigate female-inflected modes of insight and intentionality while at the same time safeguarding its epistemic guarantee as a valid form of expression.

Kane's *Cleansed* takes place in a world of internalised gazes and tight surveillance, more austere than the *Augustine*'s surroundings at the Salpêtrière. Furse reads Hysteria as the locus of the female body's freedom to construct a language, as a form of unrestrained utterance. Augustine is seen mimicking the prototypical symptom of hysteria, namely asphyxiation depicted as the 'suffocating womb' (Wald, 2007).

> **AUGUSTINE** There's something [...] pulling my tongue something in my throat...MAMAN!!!

As a patient at the Salpêtrière under the supervision of Docteur Charcot, Augustine's body is transformed into a spectacle for the benefit of his exclusively male audience. The play gives us a world of deliberative playacting and non-verbal repertoire where Augustine was subjected to various fashionable treatments of the time such as the insertion into her uterus of ovarian compressors and other contraptions, the subcutaneous administration of amyl nitrate and chloroform which only briefly suppressed her symptoms.

Furse transforms the body of the Hysteric into a topos of rebellion, a return to a savage, pre-Oedipal state unbounded by the normative taxonomies of the Symbolic Order. Docteur Charcot is shown taking his patient through a visual choreography of her symptomatology despite her initial resistance.

> *Her bed is rolled on and she is laid down on it, protesting.*

> **AUGUSTINE** OH NO! Monsieur Charcot! Not you again!

(38-40)

> **CHARCOT** Now I want you to appreciate especially the unfolding of the attack [...] So, we will use the little hysterogenic point to provoke an attack as a form of therapy

Hysteria in Performance: The subversive potential of performative malady

AUGUSTINE Dirty…beast…pig! Pig! I'll tell papa!… Put that snake back in your trousers!

She puts her hand in her mouth and as if to take something out. She holds the invisible thing on the palm of her hand and she spits on it.

Furse's Augustine escapes the confines of the Hospital and is shown returning to the Salpêtrière for a final confession but this time sartorially transformed into a man, formally reneging on her staged femininity and assuming the exterior of the Father: "I will disappear. Dis-membered. I will return. Re-membered… and you, you will put your tools down, you will listen, really listen, and you will believe every word I say…" (92). Augustine leaves the stage having engaged in her own performance, re-baptised, dis-membered by Charcot's ovarian compressors, freed from somatic constrictions and re-membered within the regulatory permissiveness of masculinity on her own terms.

In Greek tragedy, Aeschylus' hyperbolic construction of Clytemnestra in the *Oresteia* merits serious consideration. Aeschylus' construction of the Argive queen as a masterful embodiment of a female straddling the boundaries of gender is irresistible. Clytemnestra is the first female character in tragedy explicitly to problematise the split female body in both its capacities: the private sphere of the woman whose wandering womb enables a frightful reassignment of public roles and the public body of the queen/king as an un-gendered entity in whom is vested political and religious authority. Clytemnestra's journey in the *Agamemnon* starts just as Agamemnon himself is about to reappear, fresh from his Trojan spoils, while Clytemnestra has been assuming the duties of the body politic in his absence during which she amused herself with the king's cousin, Aegisthus. On Agamemnon's return we see the body of the queen enact a dual performance of masterful rhetoric silencing the Argives, the Elders, the Chorus and ending with the murder of Agamemnon by her own sword.

Her opening address on seeing the victor/husband bestride the threshold of their Argive palace confounds the public and the private through the use of its own guerrilla tactics by mixing male oratory persuasion and female ritual language: ἄνδρες πολῖται, πρέσβος Ἀργείων τόδε, (Men. Citizens. Elders of Argos. (855). The irony of the utterance "Men" against the long monologue that follows is a deliberate play of duplicitous statesmanship, an Irigarayan mimicry of the highest altitude. The middle part of the *Agamemnon* is replete with obfuscation of the boundary between male and female, replete with hyperbolic repetition, a play between the acceptable and the unacceptable.

Hysteria in Performance: The subversive potential of performative malady

At 1378 of the Agamemnon Clytemnestra announces to us she has slaughtered the Argive king. The deed was "contrived to leave no fissure" (1380), she reassures us. In any other context, the mathematical precision of this announcement would have been ascribed to a literary madwoman. Her monologue is a bloodied vista recounting the murder in all its vengeful glory: She lay a net, she tells us: ἄπειρον ἀμφίβληστρον, ὥσπερ ἰχθύων, περιστιχίζω. (1383-4) (with this vast net as may be cast for fish, I sieged him round in the fatal wealth of purple). The once arrogant chieftain of the Achaean army is no more: We have no need for stage directions; Clytemnestra's gestural outburst, we can imagine would have been one to match her verbal hyperbole.[11]

The chorus is shocked. They draw attention to the linguistic advantage of Speech (γλῶσσαν) having in Greek the dual meaning of tongue and utterance as a constituent of logos and thus not the property of a woman: θαυμάζομέν σου γλῶσσαν, ὡς θρασύστομος, / ἥτις τοιόνδ' ἐπ' ἀνδρὶ κομπάζεις λόγον (1399-1400) (I marvel at your tongue/words so brazen-bold). But Clytemnestra undercuts the argument re-appropriating the space now occupied by the dead body of the king: "Wouldst fright me, like a witless woman ? Lo, / This bosom shakes not…" (οὗτός ἐστιν Ἀγαμέμνων) "This is Agamemnon, / My husband, dead by my right hand, A most incoherent unfolding delivered through a perfectly coherent act": ἔργον δικαίας τέκτονος (1406) (A just artificer), is the work of her right hand. The two constituents of *logos*, Justice and Truth united inside Clytemnestra's right fist: τάδ' ὧδ' ἔχει (1406): "That is the truth," is her final verdict. Aeschylus delivers a female character intentionally using her corporeality to straddle the borders between logos and a-logos but equally aware of her femininity as matter subsisting as the very essence, the very being of language; she is fully adept at deploying both.

To a theatre audience already susceptible to the practices of hyperbole and metaphor, the Hysteric body in all its metaphoric exaggeration is irresistible. It is precisely this non-topological centre of mimetic symbolism that opens up a space of linguistic possibility freed from the rules of conventional grammar. If as Irigaray says, "Hysteria is all she has left" (Irigaray, 1985a, p.71), Clytemnestra is using it with strategic precision.

Shakespeare's tragedies are also replete with Elizabethan Hysterics, more so men than women which also serves to highlight the overreaching possibilities of theatrical exaggeration freed from gendered limitations as we see in the tragedy of *King Lear*. Written shortly after the death of

---

[11] οὕτω τὸν αὑτοῦ θυμὸν ὁρμαίνει πεσών, / κἀκφυσιῶν ὀξεῖαν αἵματος σφαγὴν βάλλει μ' ἐρεμνῇ ψακάδι φοινίας δρόσου, χαίρουσαν οὐδὲν ἧσσον At 1388-91 The repetitive use of the fricative, s, in her bloodied description of the slaughter, combined with the unvoiced labial π (p) accentuates the conspiratorial and menacing character of her confession, almost a whisper in our ear.

Elizabeth I, *King Lear*'s world is heavily nuanced by the anxieties of the issue of unresolved succession and the theorisation of Elizabeth's body, similar to Clytemnestra's, as the split locus of the immortal body politic of the Sovereign and her woman's body natural very much in need of a proprietor. Elizabeth's obstinate insistence on not providing one safeguarded her own sovereignty but at the same time opened up a hysterical-ly symptomatic debate about the logic (or non-) of her desire to abstain where it would have been logically natural to proceed in a conventionally Oedipal structure of continuation. Much of the drama written during her long reign is informed by this problematic with different factions deploying theatre as their forum for exposing self-serving arguments. In King Lear it is Lear himself who is the Hysteric. In Act II Sc iv, 56 we see him suffocating in emotion which he cannot logically explain nor repress. He then proceeds to find inside himself something unprecedented in the canon: a womb and what is more, a wandering womb which he intercepts swelling up towards his heart. "*Hysterica passio*, thou climbing sorrow! / Thy element's below. Where is this daughter?" Hysteria, a woman inside Lear, one that refuses to stay in her place and goes on walkabout surging up threatening to kill him, only she is in the centre of him and the Sovereign cannot suppress her. The storm, a woman standing inside the king for "the eternal irony of the community of men" (Irigaray, 1985a, p.152). The tidiness of unquestioned governability of his kingdom has been de-centred by her who is in the centre of him, disabling the comforting primacy that his manhood has provided him with and he cannot even get rid of her.

Why can he not get rid of her? Is she so necessary? It shouldn't be so, as female matter, unformed, has historically been the reference point of exclusion. On Irigaray's account Hysterical materialisation shows that the Hysteric's body by exceeding the boundaries of discourse may be outside language but it also constitutes the very "matter" of language. Lear cannot get rid of her because she precedes him; he is predicated by her, she is *being* prior to *becoming*.

In the recent feminist canon Simone de Beauvoir in her ontological discussion of femininity in *The Second Sex*, claims that "one is not born a woman but rather becomes one" (de Beauvoir, 1997) which suggests a never-ending discursive process shaped and standardised by a coded system of power relations. Given that the process of becoming in the female is not directed towards a *telos*, the metaphysical category of *Being* does not hold. Plato's cosmological account of the generation of the Universe in the *Timaeus* legitimises the condition of possibility of that which exceeds representation but concomitantly acts as the enactment of the very eidetic reason of *being* woman and operating as a third category outside the two designated categories of *Being* and *Becoming*, of the privileged place of the Hysteric's utterance as mimesis irreducible to silence, as a material substratum between the coded systems of discourse and the female character's paralysed desire. The substratum assigned to the 'third kind', the receptacle in the *Timaeus*, can provide a metaphysical explanation as to whether Hysteria, as unintelligible utterance, excluded from discursive coherence, is not merely the third cause beside *Being* and *Becoming* but positioned inside the function of the receptacle, it yields a formal space where all things must be located. Plato's anxieties about statements and predication in the late dialogues validate the metaphysical argument of placing what might have been thought of as unintelligible matter at the cusp of sensible and intelligible.

Broadly speaking, the semantics of the verb *εἶναι* (to be) combine three senses: existential, predicative (to be is to be F) and veridical (to be is to be the case). We can easily discount the existential sense of the verb here and determine that in the *Timaeus* for a thing to be is to be F and never to become in the predicative sense or in an unqualified way: to be is to be intelligible and changeless. In the *Timaeus*'s cosmological account the Universe is the craft of a Demiurge who is in charge of creating an imitation, a copy of an eternal Form. Platonic Idealism here rules that "Some things are, without ever becoming (27d6) and for such things to be then they must be grasped by understanding involving a rational account" (28a1). Perceivability belongs to the lower ranks associated with becoming. The challenge of the Demiurge in the *Timaeus* is to produce a three-dimensional set within the constraints of *becoming*, a tangible, visible, sensually perceivable model. This three-dimensional field is termed the *ὑποδοχή* (Ypodokhe), the receptacle (49a5) of all becoming or as he later calls it, the chora; the space (52a8d3).

The limitations attributable to the *τρίτον γένος* (third kind) of the Platonic chora in the *Timaeus* are obscure indeed. A material substratum, *ἕδρα* (seat) (52b1) securing a spatial location for things to enter into and disappear from it. The introduction of the chora is a significant innovation in Plato's middle metaphysics. The enduring conversations on whether the chora is conceived of as matter or space will not be resolved in this essay but I must draw attention to *Timaeus*'s 51a and 49e in support of the argument that choric emplacement is a mode of being through the characteristics of stability and permanence Plato attributes to her. He says chora is *ἀεί ὄν* (permanent / stable being) referred to as *τῷδε* (that) as opposed to a mere resembling or a copy, *τοιοῦτον* (such). His use of the noun *Χῶρα* (chora) as a female gendered noun in Greek is deliberate.

Where Irigaray liberates performative Hysteria from its predicative function, Plato situates its metaphysical *analogon*, the Chora, beyond standard philosophical discourse, chora comes before

Hysteria in Performance: The subversive potential of performative malady

the cosmos. It is not constrained by the rules of materiality because it precedes materiality; an extensible, observable space not bound by the limitations of *becoming*. Bernard Freyberg in *Provocative Form in Plato, Kant, Nietzsche (and Others)* reads Platonic Being as intelligible Form and the receptacle as anti-Form. Chora is beyond all being, an inaugural tabula rasa of inscription beyond being, a primary constituent, a pre-requisite on Irigaray's reading for all material linguistic perception which by virtue of its abyssal 'situation', is permitted to introduce a mimetic determination. It transcends being but is not reducible to sense, tangibility or matter.

Irigarayan mimicry or Platonic mimesis, the hyperbolic utterance not reducible to the particulars of matter now becomes a syntactical precondition; a necessary revelation of that which signifies materiality beyond perceivable space, unbound by the constrictions of syntactical permissibility because it precedes it. More particularly, a split or double consciousness which is a requirement for the suspension of disbelief also serves the purpose of procuring the Hysteric with the full arsenal of Hysteria. The very notion of a playwright's duty to write "the voice of a woman" locates the debate within a given scenographic perspective.

Consequently, as a dramatic character the Hysteric instantiates the dis-ease not by re-enacting the somatic trauma but by somatically transforming trauma into matter. Performative Hysteria cripples the determinate system of signs by imposing an indeterminate system of unreadability on the generating process of the performer, the spectator and ultimately the text. Any broad understanding of the receptivity of a member of a theatre audience points to the latter's ability to 'perceive' and process a theatrical 'speech Act' or what has been contentiously named by Austin an 'infelicitous' or 'a non-serious Speech Act' actualised during theatrical performances. I argue that it is precisely this infinite citationality, the rehearsed model and the repetition of the iterable which renders the performance of Hysteria a particularly relevant model of theatrical expression. Theatre performance must precisely adhere to the rules of doubleness, of rehearsed behaviour if it is to be theatrically textualised at all. The audience's awareness of this ritual of repeatability and rehearseability initiates the split awareness of witnessing 'performed' performance while simultaneously being aware of its intentionality in the body of the performer as well as within the text. Is it the transmigration of a societal and linguistic phenomenon to a topos of embodied performance medicine to combat its symptoms? Is *logos* the medicine to soothe the Hysteric and bring her back within the confines of reason? It is fitting to leave the last word to Jacques Derrida and his pharmaco-logical flirtations with the Platonic corpus. In the *Symposium*'s Platonic theatre it is Master Socrates himself who is for Derrida a *pharmakeus* par excellence, a sorcerer, a seducer and a procurer of the poison/medicine. Socrates, the son of the midwife Phaenarete, breaches the boundaries of acceptable discourse and assumes the maieutic role of his midwife/mother; Socrates, under Alcibiades' irresistible gaze becomes a piper (*Αὐλητής*) without a pipe (*ἄνευ ὀργανου*). Similarly to Furse's *Augustine*, Socrates becomes his own instrument, his own spectacle. The power of performative Hysteria is undiminished: Augustine managed to escape the confines of the Salpêtrière and come back dis-membered but re-membered. The Master logician of Western reason, dis-membered by Athenian hemlock, will not cease to show us how by crippling the determinate system of Athenian laws/signs he imposes his own indeterminate system of Socratic logic: he deploys hyperbole, playacting (*ὑποκρισια*) and comedy (*ἔιρων*) as a means of bewitching his interlocutors. Socratic theatre knows no bounds and no gender. By appropriating female space he validates its power.

Despite Plato's reservations, his own dialogical theatre unfolds before us in all its Bacchic fury. The play in Plato re-written and de-constructed by both Irigaray and Derrida, the vicissitudes between beauty and truth, between rigour and instability between the *Pharmakon* as the antidote against dramatic mimesis and the harmful activity of the demagogue/*pharmakeus* in the *Republic* sets the scene for Derrida's un-doing of the structurality of Western metaphysical discourse. The *pharmakon*, the medicine against Hysteria is *logos* but *logos* within itself carries the pernicious possibilities of phenomenal bodies transcending their assigned corporeality and redefining the conditions of representation. The *pharmakon*, in all its mirroring potentiality can, through performative mimesis, re-assign, imitate, delineate the circularity of female desire, perhaps even ultimately liberate it.

BIBLIOGRAPHY

Adleman, J., 1992. *Suffocating Mothers*. New York: Routledge.

Aeschylus, 2004. *Aeschylus, The Oresteia*. Knopf A. A., ed. Translated by J. Thompson. London: Everyman's Library.

Aeschylus, 1978. *Aeschylis Tragediae Vol IV, Lipsiae, Athens Papadimas*.

Aston, E., 1999. *Feminist Theatre Practice: A Handbook*. London: Routledge.

Austin, J., 1976. *How to Do Things with Words*. London: Oxford University Press.

Butler, J., 2008. *Gender Trouble*. New York: Routledge.

de Beauvoir, S., 1997. *The Second Sex*. Copyright Gallimard. London: Vintage.

Foley, H., 2001. *Female Acts in Greek Tragedy*. Oxford: Princeton University Press.

Freydberg, B., 2000. *Provocative Form in Plato, Kant , Nietzsche (and Others)*. New York: Lang.

Freud, S., 1909 [1908]. *Allgemeines Über den Hysterischen Anfall*. [e-book] Available through: http://www.textlog.de/freud-psychoanalyse-hysterischen-anfall.html.

Freud, S., 1893-1909 *Gesammelte Werke, Klinische Symptomatologie der Angstneurose*. [e-book] Available through: http://www.textlog.de/freud-psychoanalyse-klinische-symptomatologie-angstneurose. html.

Furse, A., 1997. *Augustine (Big Hysteria)*. Amsterdam: Harwood Academic Publishers.

Irigaray, L., 1984. *Éthique de la Différance Sexuelle*. Paris: Éditions de Minuit.

Irigaray, L., 1985. *Speculum of the Other Woman*. Translated by G. C. Gill. Ithaca: Cornell University Press.

Irigaray L., 1985a. *This Sex Which is not One*. Translated by C. Porter. Ithaca: Cornell University Press.

Kane, S., 2001. *Sarah Kane Complete Plays*. London: Methuen.

Kristeva, J., 1977. Polylogue. Paris: Seuil.

Plato, 1977. *Republic, Platonis Dialogi. Vol. IV, Lipsiae, Athens Papadimas.*

Plato, 1977. *Phaedrus, Platonis Dialogi. Vol. IV, Lipsiae, Athens Papadimas.*

Plato, 1977. *Timaeus, Platonis Dialogi. Vol. IV, Lipsiae, Athens Papadimas.*

Shakespeare, W., 1997. *King Lear (The Arden Shakespeare)* Foakes, R. A. ed. 3rd revised ed. London: Bloomsbury.

DICTIONARIES

For all translations from Classical Greek

Oxford University Press, 2001. *Oxford Grammar of Classical Greek.* Oxford: Oxford University Press.

Oxford University Press, 2002. *Oxford Classical Greek Dictionary.* Oxford: Oxford University Press.

Papanikolaou, G., 1985. *Dictionary of Classical Greek Verbs.* Athens: Papadimas.

My Mother Said by Durre Mughal

Your skin is the most revealing

part of you. But sometimes your eyes

reveal more. Yet suggestion, which

lies in your eyes and in the cloth

that swathes your skin. Just enough

for those who look to see. And not

for everyone to look and see.

Does more than your skin can.

But I say a little is

singing with the sound off.

And a lot is like being pulled

out of her womb.

So I show more than a little,

and let the cloth cover my flesh

just enough for those who look

to see. And not for everyone

to look and see.

And when it is all on, and I stand

in my own skin, I push my chin up,

straighten my shoulders. I let my eyes

wander.

I am the only one who knows

what is under this cloth,

under this dress,

under these shoes,

under the red paint of my toes.

Contributors

Cath Bore is a writer of fiction and fact, published in the UK and US. Her flash fiction can be found, amongst other places, in National Flash Fiction Day anthologies 2014 and 2015, Flash Fiction Magazine and the first three Slim Volume books (Pankhearst Publishing, 2015). She is also a panellist for Bay TV's 52% programme, and writes about pop culture and music for webzine Get Into This. Based in Merseyside UK, she has an MA in Creative Writing from Liverpool John Moores University. Cath is currently completing a crime novel. Her blog is at https://cathbore.wordpress.com/ You can find her on Twitter at @cathbore

Susan Dunsford is a Brit living abroad. She grew up in England and had a highly conventional life which involved a typical degree, a safe career, a husband, a child and a mortgage. Nearly a decade ago she became a trailing spouse and moved to the American Midwest. Having studied an MA in Women's and Gender Studies, she is passionate about equality, diversity and justice. She also loves teaching, reading, writing, baking, walking and just lazing around having fun. There's probably some wine drinking and movie watching in there as well. Influences include Simone de Beauvoir, Judith Butler and Dona Haraway. She reads almost anything from The Canterbury Tales to The Hunger Games and watches an absurd amount of superhero movies. Susan fully intends to become a mad cat lady when she's older, and has plans to be a grumpy old woman who glares at the neighbours. For now she is a typical middle-aged mother and teacher, who secretly nurtures a subversive mind of her own.

Erika Garrett is a single mother with three children and a paranoid cat. She campaigns for abortion clinic buffer zones and runs @womentogether, a project that focuses on supporting women affected by UK government cuts.

Lorrie Hartshorn is a contemporary and literary fiction writer, whose work has been featured in a number of journals, including Compose, Paraxis, 1000 Words, The Pygmy Giant and Anthem. She is the founder of Halo Literary Magazine, a new journal of short fiction by women and blogs at Circles Under Streetlights (circlesunderstreetlights.wordpress.com)

Claire Heuchan is a Black radical feminist from Scotland. At the time of publication, she is working towards attaining her MLitt in Gender Studies – the focus of her research is Black feminist theory, activism, and writing. Claire volunteers at Glasgow Women's Library, and is a proud member of their organisational team for Collect:If, a networking group by and for creative women of colour in Scotland.

Claire blogs as Sister Outrider, and has been published by platforms such as Media Diversified and Feminist Current. Her ongoing research projects the self-definition of Black womanhood within African American women's autobiographies, and the means by which the politics of identity manifest in the poetry of Black Scottish women. Claire's research degree commences in October. Follow Claire on twitter : @ClaireShrugged

Priscilla Lugo I'm a social justice advocate, a feminist, and a Chicana. I come from a border town in south Texas, where more than 90% of the population is Hispanic. I'm the daughter of immigrant parents who come from Aguascalientes, Durango, and Nuevo Laredo, Mexico. My parents sacrificed everything and worked tooth and nail to make sure my siblings and I had everything we could have ever wanted. It is through their experiences and my experiences as a woman, Chicana, and feminist that I draw on to inspire me to help me write and help others. I'm currently a sophomore at The University of Texas at Austin pursuing a major in English and a minor in Women and Gender Studies. After graduating in 2019 I plan on going into the nonprofit world and helping women receive an education in third world countries or helping advance immigrants rights here in the United States.

I also write for a blog, latinx4change.blogspot.com where we write about the struggles the Latinx community faces. I'm also an enormous fan of Harry Potter, John Green, and a lover of all literature. My guilty pleasures include YA novels, anything Beyoncé, and social media. My current favorite book is "milk and honey" by Rupi Kaur. I like to write poetry in my spare time and I'm currently writing a book about the struggles women and minorities face in the day and age of institutionalized racism and rampant sexism.

Lucy Middlemass contributed short stories to three Pankhearst YA collections, Heathers, Mermaids and Moremaids, and is a senior editor at Pankhearst. She wrote the Kindle single Mothers, and co-authored a second single, Convertible. She also contributed a short story to For Books' Sake's [Re]Sisters, and co-authored the YA collection First Girl On The Moon. She reads a lot of YA and radical feminism, and would like to see them together more often. Lucy offers editing services through We Are Furious https://wearefurious.wordpress.com/ and can be found on Twitter @LucyMiddlemass

Durre Mughal writes fiction, non-fiction and poetry about gender, ethnicity, and mental health. Her writing was shortlisted for The Robin Reeves Prize for Young Writers and was published in the anthology How To Exit a Burning Building (2015). She has been published in the anthology Metropolitan Volume 1 (2015), The Stockholm Review of Literature and in the upcoming issues of Halo Lit Mag and Severine Lit. She has an MA in Creative Writing and hopes to do a PhD in the near future. She is a regular contributor to Wales Arts Review and can be found on Twitter or on her Blog.

Estella Muzito is an avid reader of stories and non-fiction. She is passionate about the rights of girls and women. This inspires her view of the world. Estella found her voice in a blog, unculturedsisterhood - and is the first to admit that she needs to make time to keep it going. She is Ugandan, lives in Kampala and tweets @EstellaMz

Egoyibo Okoro is a Nigerian lawyer, postcolonial feminist and creative thinker. She is currently enrolled in a (double degree) Master's program in Women's & Gender Studies at Utrecht University, the Netherlands and University of Hull, UK. A lover of the literary word, Egoyibo is a voracious reader who is passionate about human rights, feminism, social good and justice.

Poppy O'Neill is a writer of short and flash fiction. Her work has been featured in Aesthetica, The Mother, Mslexia and Halo Literary Magazine. She is currently writing her first novel.
Born and raised in the salty air of coastal Sussex, Poppy studied for her BA in creative writing in the beautiful surroundings of Bretton Hall, part of the University of Leeds. She then went on to study a PGCert in journalism at the University of the Arts, London.
After three years working in fashion, she returned to writing and now runs the Fountain Pen writing group, who meet monthly in a local pub. She also founded an online feminist book club aimed at giving women new to feminism a grounding in the literature of the movement. By day she works in communications for a tech company. Poppy lives in Chichester with her husband and two children and will be starting her MA at the University of Chichester in the autumn. She enjoys reading, dancing and righteous feminist anger.

Sunayna Pal was born in Mumbai, moved to USA after marriage. She has PG degrees from XLRI and Annamalai University and worked in the Corporate World for five odd years and realized that this is not what she wanted to do. She broke the chains of education and Corporate world to embark on her heart's pursuits. She started "Art with Sunayna" (artwithsunayna.wordpress.com) to teach and sell art for NGOs and became a certified handwriting analyst (sos4graphology.com) to help people understand themselves better by using a mix of graphotherapy, healing and affirmations.

In the midst of all this and being a new mother, who loves gardening and photography, she also likes to write from her daily life experiences. Many of her articles have been published in TOI, New woman, Women's era and she is a proud contributor at many other e-magazines and sites. Many of her stories are published in anthologies like "Mighty Thoughts," "The second Life," "Memoirs of Love," "Rhymes and Rhythm," "Voice of Little Hearts," and few are published in international anthologies like "Nepal - An awakening", "The Collaborative's Omnibus" and "Soaring High".

She is currently working on an anthology of 51 stories of people who are of South Asian origin and have an experience to share of USA. In her little spare time, she also maintains a blog at mannkiwindow.wordpress.com and can be contacted at sunayna.pal@gmail.com

Louise Pennington is a feminist writer and activist who has published articles in Role/Reboot, New Statesman, New Internationalist and JumpMag. Louise works as the media analyst for the campaign organisation Everyday Victim Blaming, which challenges media misrepresentations of domestic and sexual violence. She created EVB Press to raise funds for *Everyday Victim Blaming* and has already published a collection of essays, short stories and two poetry anthologies. EVB Press has since branched out into publishing feminist and womanist writing. She founded *A Room of Our Own: A Feminist & Womanist Network* to celebrate women writers as part of her commitment to ending cultural femicide. When she's not writing or railing against the Patriarchy, Louise can be found at Superhero conventions with her kids and trying to herd cats.

Effie Samara was born in Athens and raised in the village of Caversham in Berkshire. She read Law at Reading University and Creative Writing at Cambridge. She is currently a doctoral researcher at Glasgow University where she explores Meta-Exile: Revolutionary Dramaturgies for Female Characters in exilic British and Irish Drama. She has worked extensively on the question of theatre as a discursive intersection and on the idea of Movement patterns vesting the woman exile with a revolutionary leap towards a poeisis, a poetic creation which transcends the constrictive conditions of exile. She has made contributions on the concepts of "exilic transcendence" and Hegel's historical consciousness reinterpreted as a female weapon towards the formation of revolutionary theatrical and political representations.

Her theatre work includes Bad Girl, BABY (The Hope Theatre), A Brief History of the World Written by a Lady of Conviction (BREAD AND ROSES THEATRE) SARTRE (directed by Michael Langridge). She is presently working on two theatre projects; The Irish Revolution, a One-Act play, which examines the inflammatory abortion debates across Europe and America, and she is also under commission to develop LESBOS, a play about the dynamics of the present female exodus into Europe. Her plays examine how theatrical practices are able to provide a map for revolutionary action against the motionless apparatus of static dramaturgy and an anti-discourse against the negative semantics implicitly attached to women's histories by generating narrative strategies for politicising and representing the nomadic woman.

Effie is proudly mum to a fierce little goddess.

Millie Slavidou Millie Slavidou is a writer and translator. She is the author of the Instaexplorer series for pre-teens, a grammar handbook aimed at parents and she is also known for her articles on linguistics. She lives in Greece with her three children, where she is currently researching her book on etymology.

Printed in Great Britain
by Amazon